W9-ABP-242

Date Due

OCT 12			
OCT 26			
MAY 30			
APR 30			
		WITHDRAWN	

Demco-293

The Aquinas Lecture, 1962

THE LURE
OF WISDOM

Under the Auspices of Wisconsin-Alpha
Chapter of the Phi Sigma Tau

by

JAMES D. COLLINS, Ph.D.

MARQUETTE UNIVERSITY PRESS
MILWAUKEE
1962

Library of Congress Catalog Card Number: 62-13514

© Copyright 1962
By the Wisconsin-Alpha Chapter
of the Phi Sigma Tau
Marquette University

PRINTED
IN
U. S. A.

BD
181
C65

6·25·62

2.09

MARQUETTE UNIV.

78123

*To Violet Stafford
and to the Memory of
Dr. Leo J. Stafford*

Prefatory

The Wisconsin-Alpha Chapter of the Phi Sigma Tau, National Honor Society for Philosophy at Marquette University, each year invites a scholar to deliver a lecture in honor of St. Thomas Aquinas. Customarily delivered on a Sunday close to March 7, the feast day of the Society's patron saint, the lectures are called the Aquinas Lectures.

In 1962 the Aquinas Lecture "The Lure of Wisdom" was delivered on March 11 in the Peter A. Brooks Memorial Union of Marquette University by Dr. James D. Collins, professor of philosophy, St. Louis University.

Dr. Collins was born in Holyoke, Massachusetts on July 12, 1917. He received his A.B. degree from Catholic University of America in 1941. In 1942 he received his A.M. degree and in 1944 his Ph.D. degree also from Catholic University of America. After a year as research fellow in philosophy at Harvard University he came to St. Louis University in 1945.

He is a former president of the American Catholic Philosophical Association, a member of the American Philosophical Association, and Phi Beta Kappa. He is currently president of the Metaphysical Society of America.

His published books include *The Thomistic Philosophy of the Angels* (Washington, D.C.: Catholic University of America Press, 1947); *The Existentialists: A Critical Study* (Chicago: Regnery, 1952); *The Mind of Kierkegaard* (Chicago: Regnery, 1953); *A History of Modern European Philosophy* (Milwaukee: Bruce Publishing Co., 1954); *God in Modern Philosophy* (Chicago: Regnery, 1959).

In addition, he served as editor of *Philosophical Readings in Cardinal Newman* (Chicago: Regnery, 1961) and is a contributor to *The Modern Schoolman, The New Scholasticism, The Thomist, International Philosophical Quarterly, Journal of Philosophy, Review of Metaphysics, Philosophical Review, Giornale di Metafisica, Thought* and *Cross Currents.*

To these books and many articles in learned journals, Phi Sigma Tau has the pleasure of adding *The Lure of Wisdom.*

The Lure of Wisdom

It is sometimes assumed that philosophical concern about attaining to wisdom was confined to the ancient and medieval worlds, and that this aim withered away as one of the chief casualties of the waning Middle Ages. On this view, the modern philosophers do no more than make a customary etymological bow in the direction of the love and pursuit of wisdom, while actually organizing their thought around methods and themes which cannot yield, and are not intended to yield, wisdom as their proper fruit. The practical consequence of reading history in this way is to conclude that contemporary minds have no business in bothering about wisdom. If men persist in searching after it with philosophical instruments, then they must pay the price either of attempting an impossible throwback to a past civilization or else of breaking so completely with the whole

trend of modern speculation that their
views are freakish and unattractive to the
contemporary mind.

I do not think that the present-day
prospects for wisdom are quite so desper-
ate or that the history of modern positions
on wisdom has been properly investigated.
The more we probe comparatively into
modern philosophy, the more striking is
seen to be the persistence of the basic
themes from one age to another. Wisdom
being one of these basic topics in philosophy, it seems antecedently unlikely that
it should be an extraordinary exception to
this historical continuity, unless one were
to define it so narrowly as to bind it down
to just one philosophical theory about wisdom or one cultural situation for its appearance. And when we turn to the actual
texts of the modern philosophers, we find
that this antecedent unlikelihood of its dis-
appearance is borne out by the actual discussions of wisdom undertaken by these
thinkers. Their writings show that wisdom
is not shunted aside as lacking in interest
or as impossible of attainment. Rather, it

is treated in new ways and integrated with new conceptions concerning the human mind and the goals of human life. The historical record shows that it does continue to engage modern philosophers as providing one of their proper topics and aims of philosophizing. Unless we attend to what they say about the meaning and accessibility of wisdom, we will be overlooking an important strain in modern philosophy and thus depriving ourselves of some relevant guidance on the ways to approach wisdom in our own age.

Our net cannot reach out far enough to snare all the aspects of this vast question of how wisdom has fared at the hands of the modern philosophers. But at least a start can be made by investigating three relevant points. Our first task will be to notice how the problem of wisdom came to a head with the Skeptics and Stoics of the later Renaissance, thus forming a major part of the heritage of problems accepted in modern philosophy. The next step will be to study in some detail the conception of wisdom proposed by Descartes, since this constitutes one of the fundamental modern orientations on the whole matter. And finally, these historical indications will be put to work in the analysis of a few contemporary aspects of the problem of wisdom. The historical perspective may help us to recognize some particular ways in which to clarify and strengthen the love of wisdom today.

Historical and contemporary considerations are deliberately intermingled here in order to bring out, in a specific instance, the mutual dependence and fruitful intercourse between the study of past thinkers and the intelligent appraisal of contemporary viewpoints. The value of such an interplay is sometimes doubted in times of social crisis and swift succession of scientific theories. But even under these conditions, philosophizing retains its distinctive structure, an unavoidably complex one which must involve a living study of history as well as a responsiveness to current approaches. On this issue, a sound observation made by an investigator in another field holds equally well for philosophy. Karl Rahner suggests that "we should enter into association with a thinker of the past, not only to become acquainted with his views but in the last resort to learn something about reality."[1] Historical association helps to familiarize ourselves with reality not only in a general and timeless way but also in terms of the look it has in our own day, since that look is shaped by the problems and methods placed at our disposal by past thinkers. That this relationship holds in the case of wisdom is a guiding consideration in the present study.

1. WISDOM AMONG THE CHRISTIAN STOICS AND SKEPTICS

As the Renaissance drew to its close in the later sixteenth century, it brought to the exploding point a crisis concerning wisdom. This crisis had been slowly brewing during the transitional centuries of the early modern world, when so many elements in the medieval outlook were being

1. Karl Rahner, S.J., *Theological Investigations* (Baltimore: Helicon Press, 1961), I, 10.

revised and sometimes deeply transformed.[2] The new conceptions about man,
the material universe, and religious revelation could scarcely leave unaffected the
long tradition on wisdom. Once the
changes set in with respect to these other
areas, they were bound to raise some new
questions concerning the wisdom ideal
which depended so intimately upon the
predominant way of conceiving man and
the world in relation to God. This ideal
could not be insulated and kept unaltered
except at the price of cutting it off from its
roots of nourishment in the actual concerns
of men.

From a reading of the Scholastic manuals used in the colleges, it is true, one
would not be struck vividly by the ferment

2. E. F. Rice, *The Renaissance Idea of Wisdom*
   (Cambridge, Mass.: Harvard University Press,
   1958), gives a conspectus of the humanist, Prot-
   estant, and Stoic views, with a culminating chapter on Pierre Charron (pp. 178-207). His conclusion about the Renaissance drift toward a
   naturalization of the idea of wisdom is marred,
   however, by his oversimplified notion of the medieval positions, which contain more practical
   and moral elements of wisdom than Rice allows.

surrounding the concept of wisdom. They continued in a placid way to enumerate Aristotle's traits of the wise man, to deal with wisdom as the highest intellectual virtue, and to differentiate between metaphysical wisdom and the wisdoms which come from the gift of the Holy Spirit and the study of theology. Indirectly, however, this very repetition of the traditional teaching might evoke some concern on the part of an alert reader who was also familiar with the work currently being done by the later Renaissance representatives of the Stoic and Skeptical schools. For, on all these aspects of the topic of wisdom, there was sufficient discussion and reformulation going on in the Renaissance age to merit following a less routine procedure. The doctrine on wisdom was actually in course of being returned to the status of a question open for dispute and ready for some solutions which diverged considerably from the usual presentations.

The two main proponents of Christian Stoicism, Guillaume Du Vair and Justus Lipsius, regarded their work as a new advance rather than as an antiquarian excursion into the Greek past, and pointed to their theory of wisdom as justification. They felt that Christian wisdom has a power of growth and assimilation on the philosophical plane which had not been fully developed on an Aristotelian or Platonic basis, and which requires a new use of Stoic resources. The Stoic theme of the wise man appealed to them as a center for reworking some views about God and man which would better meet the needs of their own age.

Three general features in Renaissance Stoicism are directly relevant to their project of rethinking the meaning of wisdom. For one thing, Du Vair and Lipsius refrained from allying themselves with any particular school of Catholic theology but sought to modify the Stoic philosophy in the light of the Church's ordinary teaching on God and man. Their position was not motivated by antagonism toward theology but by an effort to disentangle the ideal of wisdom from particular theological disputes which might distract men from its

effective significance for their moral life.
The effect of this policy was to withdraw
the emphasis previously accorded to wisdom in its theological sense. Secondly and
by way of positive compensation for the
loss of this theological aspect of the notion
of wisdom, the Stoic thinkers stressed the
need for wisdom considered as a gift coming to men of faith from the Holy Spirit.
The religious aspect of the wisdom of the
Christian Stoics consisted in a personal reflection on human life as regulated by the
Church's common teaching on the freedom of the creative act, God's providential concern for human individuals, and
man's ordination to the life of God for his
real happiness.

The third point on which the Christian
Stoics were in agreement concerned the
need for recognizing and bringing into
prominence the practical intellectual virtue of moral wisdom. This was a place
where they saw a need for moving beyond
Aristotle, since it was partly out of respect
for his classification of the practical intellectual virtues that the Schoolmen had

hesitated about discussing a distinct virtue of moral wisdom. Both the older Stoics and the Patristic writers had viewed the wise man as one who orders his conduct in the light of some ultimate moral truths bearing on divine matters. Now, the new Stoics proposed to offer this moral wisdom as a distinctive help for men in an age already severely tried by wars and the constant pressure of a purely naturalistic view of human existence. The particular contribution of Du Vair was to study moral wisdom as a perfection of the moral-religious individual, whereas Lipsius gave his main attention to it as a perfection leading to moral philosophy.

Writing deliberately in the vernacular in order to make his moral thought more readily available to every man, Du Vair speaks about prudence, wisdom, and (in its most exalted form) sapience. Although he accepts the definition of it as the truth and knowledge of all things, principally of the divine or highest things, his chief interest lies not so much in the content of this knowledge as in the virtuous habit it-

self and its effect in prompting the moral-
religious agent toward his real goal. That
goal consists in sharing in the divine eternal wisdom, namely, the self-knowledge of
God and the truths revealed by Christ.[3]
Men can participate in this divine wisdom
in various ways and degrees, thus ac-
counting for the fact that there are several
modes of human wisdom, extending all the
way from moral judgment to the beatific
vision. Du Vair calls his view of human
participations in wisdom "the holy philosophy," in order to stress the solidarity in
principle between the wisdom of moral
prudence and that wisdom which is a religious sapience grounded in faith. We
gather our knowledge of divine things both
from the natural world and human experience and from Scripture. Hence we can
draw our image of the wise man not only
from the Stoic descriptions but also from
the sapiental books of the Old Testament
and the lives of the Desert Fathers.

3. Guillaume Du Vair, *De la Sainte philosophie
[et] Philosophie morale des stoïques*, ed. G. Mi-
chaut (Paris: Vrin, 1946), pp. 16, 20.

Du Vair focuses upon meditation as the most proper act of the human soul in this life.[4] This act involves some self-analysis but also a constant reference of one's plans to the rule of God and the finality of sharing in His eternal wisdom. From the human exemplars of wise living furnished by philosophy, Scripture, and Church tradition, we learn that a meditative hold upon our relation with the providing God is the best way to understand the human condition, endure its trials, and keep to upright resolutions. The morally and religiously wise man is the one who tenaciously orients human affairs toward God, and then develops the virtues of clemency and liberality, justice and charity. Du Vair brings out more decisively than did the older Stoics the constant struggle involved in maintaining this orientation, as well as the personal reality and personal concern of God for each of us. He likes to refer to

4. *Ibid.*, p. 51. On prudential wisdom and the passions, see G. Du Vair, *The Moral Philosophie of the Stoicks*, ed. R. Kirk (New Brunswick: Rutgers University Press, 1951), pp. 61-62, 102.

moral-religious wisdom as our shining buckler of Achilles, because it enables our mind to unmask fluctuating opinions, see with certain knowledge that all events are beneficently disposed of God, and thus arouse our eagerness for gaining a more intimate share in eternal wisdom.

On some matters, Du Vair fails to answer the questions that naturally arise in the face of his teaching. He does not establish with precision the distinctive ways in which the Christian faith, a reading of the Stoics, and his own reasoning contribute to this notion of wisdom. His shining buckler remains in the metaphorical condition. It endows him with the requisite certainty about a morally ordered universe and the direction of human freedom toward the personal God. But it does not enable him to set out for our common judgment the grounds upon which he makes these affirmations whereon the life of wisdom depends.

Lipsius, on the contrary, is deeply concerned to furnish a philosophical grounding for the theory of wisdom. There must indeed be a cleansing and adapting of secular wisdom on those issues where its Greek professors may be in conflict with revelation and Christian moral standards. But by "secular wisdom," he means quite emphatically the entire body of Stoic philosophy, with its threefold division into logic, physics, and ethics. The natural foundations of wisdom must be soundly laid in this philosophy as a whole, if anything significant is to be meant by incorporating human wisdom into the context of faith. Lipsius combs the writings of the Greek and Latin Fathers to show that they found classical Stoicism basically congenial to their Christian faith and regarded it as a deepening of both Plato's view of the good and Aristotle's vision of a law-ruled universe.[5] In particular, St. Augustine's

5. The argument for a convergence of Greek and Christian conceptions of the wise man is the form of Christian philosophy which dominates Justus Lipsius' *Manuductio ad Stoicam Philosophiam*, in his *Opera Omnia* (4 vols.: Wesel, Hoogenhuysen, 1675), IV, 613-821. In addition to St. Augustine, testimony favorable to the Stoics is drawn from such Christian authorities as Clement of Alexandria, Tertullian, Jerome, and Charles Borromeo.

testimony on the fundamental agreement of these three Greek sources concerning the liberation of the wise man from error and disturbing passions counts heavily in favor of this program for a Christian Stoic wisdom, involving some technical philosophy.

Lipsius is sensitive to the skeptical objection that the ideal of the Stoic wise man is an empty one, since we never encounter such a person in actual life. His reply rests on a distinction between two ways of viewing wisdom: terminally in the ultimate good it brings to the mind, and instrumentally in the development of definite habits of mind which serve as the proper means to the final possession of wisdom. Considered terminally or teleologi-

See *Manuductio,* book I, dissertations 17-18 (IV: 674-80). For St. Augustine's own teaching on wisdom, consult E. Gilson, *The Christian Philosophy of Saint Augustine* (New York: Random House, 1960), pp. 115-26, and V. J. Bourke, "Wisdom in the Gnoseology of Saint Augustine," *Augustinus,* III (1958), 331-36. Augustinian wisdom includes both contemplative and practical knowledge, along with a stress upon the affective love of wisdom.

cally, wisdom signifies the perfect good of
the human mind, that is, a universal
knowledge of things divine and human,
issuing in a love for God as our supreme
good. Lipsius accepts the Christian position that we do not have this fulness of
wisdom in our actual possession in this life.
Nevertheless, we can recognize it as the
supreme perfecting of our mind and can
develop those virtues which will place us
on the road toward obtaining it. The Stoic
portrait of the wise man is now explained
by Lipsius as a picture of man in his pil-
grim condition, as a concrete image of the
means we can indeed use to orient ourselves toward the terminal wisdom of God.
In this instrumental sense, wisdom is actually being realized among men of con-
stancy and sound judgment, or *bona mens.*[6]

Where Lipsius moves beyond the moralist's standpoint of Du Vair is in insisting

6.   Justus Lipsius, *Tvvo Bookes of Constancie*, ed.
R. Kirk (New Brunswick: Rutgers University
Press, 1939), pp. 137-40. J. L. Saunders outlines
the Lipsian concept of wisdom in *Justus Lipsius:
The Philosophy of Renaissance Stoicism* (New
York: Liberal Arts Press, 1955), pp. 68-86.

that the wise man should have some grounds in an elaborated philosophical system. He must be able to justify his convictions by means of an ethics which itself springs from a philosophical view of knowledge and nature. The stability of right reason which the modern Stoic seeks in moral matters results from the habit of appraising particular situations in their reference to universal divine providence. But for assurance about the immanent order in the universe and God's active, intelligent presence therein, he is reliant upon the philosophy of nature. A theory of knowledge is also required in order to understand and control our images and passions. The wisdom of the moral agent has its intellectual context, then, in the full body of Stoic philosophy.

Lipsius sometimes refers to a metaphysical wisdom, but it constitutes the peak of natural philosophy rather than a distinct science of its own. Moral philosophy depends on philosophy of nature or "physiology," especially that portion of it which deals with God and His relation

with the order of events in nature.[7] The
wise moral agent may be able to defend
his judgments informally by reflection upon his experience of human affairs, or defend them religiously by appeal to his
Christian conception of the created universe. But if his wisdom is ever to take the
form of a moral science, he must appeal
eventually to the Stoic theory of the cos-
mos and its analysis of how our mind forms
the primary notions of things and moral
goals.

This conjunction between moral wisdom and the Stoic theoretical bases of
philosophy was necessary if Christian Stoicism was to retain its philosophical stand-
ing. But it was achieved at a fateful time

7. Lipsius accommodates the Stoic theory of God
   as the active principle in the universe to the
   Christian insistence upon divine transcendence,
   in his *Physiologia Stoicorum*. See especially the
   discussion of providence and fate in book I, dissertations 3-12, where natural theology is treated
   as that part of philosophical physics dealing with
   God as the efficient principle, soul, and mind in
   nature (*Opera Omnia,* IV: 837-53). The metaphysical aspects of this work are discussed by L.
   Zanta, *La Renaissance du stoïcisme au XVIe
   siècle* (Paris: Champion, 1914), pp. 225-37.

when these bases in natural philosophy and theory of knowledge were being called into question by the Skeptics, and then subjected to deep transformations in the wake of the work done by Galileo, Descartes, and Hobbes. Their innovations concerning nature, knowledge, and human action could not leave the notion of wisdom unaltered, which means that they could not leave unscathed the view of wisdom found in Christian Stoicism.

It might be thought that the impact of modern Skepticism upon the search for wisdom would be entirely destructive, but such is not the case with Michel de Montaigne and Pierre Charron. They believed that something could be salvaged from the long wisdom tradition, even after they suspended their assent to the claims made for our rational power of demonstration concerning realities other than man. Something valuable to man would remain, even after skeptical criticism had excised the entire middle area of wisdom speculation which depended on demonstrations in speculative philosophy. There could be made an immediate junction between our basic desire for wisdom and its moral termination. As it were, the Skeptics hoped to weave directly together the initial and terminal strands in the pattern of wisdom, without committing themselves on the strength of the broad middle section. This they tried to do by emphasizing some meanings of wisdom which had been overshadowed by the previous insistence upon possessing universal certain knowledge of the highest cause of all things. If the latter claim were dropped, there would still remain some senses of wisdom which can satisfy the needs of practical living.

The fideistic Skeptics proposed that a retrenched conception of wisdom should consist of four minimal components. One of these is the whole field of wisdoms in the restricted sense which had seemed very minor in comparison with the universal types of wisdom. Even when there are conflicting views concerning the attainability of universal causal knowledge, human civilization nevertheless keeps from collapsing in virtue of the specialized competence of master statesmen, architects, physicians, and the like. Their limited wisdoms have a practical, probable import which can readily be accommodated within a skeptical framework. They give us sufficient confidence about the human mind to avoid practical despair, even though they do not provide sufficient grounds for rehabilitating metaphysics and natural philosophy. A second ingredient is the informal sort of wisdom, nonphilosophical and yet somehow speculative in nature, which we often attribute to a man of broad experience and reflective cast of mind. He can bring home to us some stubborn traits of human life, even apart from offering any practical advice about what to do in the face of them. His wisdom is usually salted away in the form of sayings and stories, which can be skeptically interpreted to refer to human phenomenal experience of change and not to the inner nature of things distinct from man.

Closely akin is the third facet of wisdom, as presented in its minimal skeptical version. This is the cast of mind proper to the moral agent, the man of prudent moral decisions who can take a large view of our practical difficulties. He is raised above mere shrewdness and technical skill by his habit of always bearing in mind the relationship of fulfillment which our moral actions must bear with our own composite nature of sensation and thinking, passion and voluntary resolve. In seeking the appropriate course of action, the man of moral wisdom will meditate upon the counsels of the Greek and Roman moralists without burdening himself with their speculative framework, and will give heed to the Christian moral ideal without expanding it into a formal theology. And finally, as these believing Skeptics of the later Renaissance and early seventeenth century envisaged the sage person, he will be a man of faith who accepts and uses the gift of wisdom coming from the Holy Spirit. It will be from this source and not from any philosophical considerations that the wise man will be inclined always to bear in mind that his ultimate goal lies in eternity, and that he can trust in God's direction of our existence thereto. This religious orientation of our practical appraisals can be maintained despite our puzzlement over theological disputes, clashing speculative philosophies, and the great diversity of customs among the tribes of men.

It was by realigning these four elements in the wisdom tradition, then, that the fideistic Skeptics sought to move from a purely suspensive position to the practical guidance of life. They offered a working wisdom which can become ours, whatever the outcome of the grand speculative disputes. To them can be traced the powerful modern conviction that a viable moral wisdom is attainable by men, even if philosophical certainty about the highest causes of all things continues to elude our grasp.

Montaigne stands athwart our path, however, lest we try to become sages too easily, even in this truncated sense. His well-known critique of the senses and natural reason assumes fresh significance, when it is taken as the negative phase in his quest for a restricted skeptical wisdom.

When his *Essays* are read in this light, they tell us that moral maxims and precepts do not really derive by necessary entailment from a knowledge which has penetrated to the intrinsic structure of the universe. The wise man must indeed follow nature and consent to nature, as the older and more recent Stoics teach, but the speculative philosophers of nature can furnish only some artificial suppositions rather than the genuine marks of natural reality. Montaigne finds his physics and his metaphysics sufficiently in the study of himself, where it is enough to analyze the pattern of his interior experience without building any ontological claims upon it. The material for prudent judgment will be furnished by a study of human inclinations, habits, and social relations. That man is created by God and destined to find his eternal happiness in the possession of God is a formative truth which faith brings him as a principle for ordering the constantly shifting experiences of men, but this truth is not the product of philosophical inference.

Montaigne mounts a sustained positive argument for a double wisdom, human and divine, which is to be synthesized only in one's personal manner of existing. The human face of wisdom does not have a foundation in any philosophical system about the world, but draws upon that common, homely acquaintance with ourselves in everyday situations which Socrates has always symbolized.[8] It teaches us to expect constant and pervasive change in all our experience and to take into account the deep influence of habit upon all our valuations and choices. In its directly moral aspect, Montaigne's human wisdom proposes but one modest imperative: be content with your own human reality and learn to enjoy it moderately under its tem-

---

8. Michel de Montaigne, "Essays," III, 12, in *The Complete Works of Montaigne*, trans. D. M. Frame (Stanford: Stanford University Press, 1957), p. 793. Montaigne has the minimal confidence that, "as she [nature] has furnished us with feet to walk with, so she has given us wisdom to guide us in life," albeit a halting human wisdom of experience. *Ibid.*, III, 13 (Frame, p. 822).

poral, composite, and habit-forming conditions.

He is suspicious of any philosophically
based maxims urging us to overcome the
passions and promising us a perfectly con-
tented and ordered life. Precisely what
human wisdom cannot achieve is the con-
stancy and order of the Stoic sage's dream.

> For all his wisdom, the sage is still a
> man: what is there more vulnerable,
> more wretched, and more null? Wis-
> dom does not overcome our natural
> limitations.[9]

We are placed on the road toward such an
overcoming of instability only by the grace
of God received through Christian faith,
and this is the special work of divine wisdom in us. The two wisdoms of humane
action and religious meditation are united
directly and exclusively through a personal
synthesis on the part of the believer.

This way of conceiving the interplay
between the wisdoms based on man and
God appeals strongly to Pascal, who also

---

9.   *Ibid.*, II, 2 (Frame, p. 249).

locates wisdom in our self-awareness of human weakness and our appeal to God for assurance about the religious view of existence. Montaigne and Pascal are engaged in methodically confining wisdom to the two moments of lucidity we achieve concerning our human condition and our religious hope of sharing hereafter in the eternal being of God. This is a personal synthesis which deliberately limits itself to humanistic reflection and the testimony of faith, with the expectation that artful description of our common human wisdom about ourselves will prepare for acceptance of the religious wisdom about the power of grace and the ultimate destiny of man. But Montaigne acknowledges that an existential split continues to remain between his super-celestial thoughts and his subterranean actions, between the religious wisdom referring his mind toward God and the wisdom of natural human contentment which actually governs his feelings and decisions. What still holds the two sides of wisdom together in his mind is the reflective religious maxim that it is proper to love life and cultivate it in the form God has given to it, that is, to respect our composite reality and not to despise our mixed condition.

A similar problem in the unity of wisdom confronts Charron at the outset of his treatise *On Wisdom*. He notes that the usual view of wisdom as a habit and type of knowledge giving sufficiency of mind in a high and unusual degree leads to a threefold division of wisdom into worldly, human, and divine. The possessors of these three wisdoms would be respectively the expert in some special field, the philosopher, and the theologian.[10] Yet Charron questions whether this division can be regarded as exhaustive, since then it would be subject to a double disadvantage. For wisdom would then be so highly professionalized that it would remain inaccessible to the ordinary meditative man, and so closely bound up with some scientific

10.   Pierre Charron, *De la Sagesse*, Preface (reprint of the 3d ed. of 1607; Paris: Feuge, 1646), pp. 5-11.

mode of knowledge that it would not spring from moral rectitude. This is clearly unsatisfactory, since we call some men wise who are not professionally trained, and since we also recognize a mutual bond between genuine wisdom and moral integrity. Hence Charron seeks to justify the notion of a generally attainable and morally based wisdom, one which indeed has the best right to be called a human wisdom. It will be located in the mind and will of the good moral agent, and will perfect him precisely as a man, not as a specialist of howsoever exalted a profession. This is the wisdom of plenary, integral prudence—*la vraye prud'hommie*—characterizing the judgments and decisions of the man who adheres to the rule of human nature or reason.

In order to insure the wisdom of the moral agent as the primary and unifying meaning, Charron critically reviews the threefold classification. His strategy is to postpone any serious considerations of the wisdoms of the worldly expert and the theologian until he has successfully recon-

stituted the basis of the middle kind of
human wisdom. This latter task involves a
transfer of human philosophical wisdom
from a speculative basis to a practical one,
and the transfer depends in turn upon an
act of detachment and then one of attach-
ment. The human mind must release itself from certitudinal acceptance of any
system of metaphysics or natural philosophy, and then freely accept those moral
teachings which will enable it to develop
a sapiental prudence in judging and acting.

So that human wisdom will no longer
mean the speculative intellectual virtue of
the metaphysician or the Stoic philosopher
of nature, Charron adopts the skeptical
position on all propositions in speculative
philosophy. He is just as remorseless as
Montaigne in taking candle and dissecting
knife to the human mind when it claims
to have certitude about how things are,
apart from the appearances in man. Yet
the unflattering skeptical view of the mind
is also the first page in the primer of moral
wisdom, and a page moreover which can
be read without depending upon any dem-

onstrative speculative philosophy. The latter can be bypassed in developing the
plenary prudence of moral wisdom in the
good man. Charron is an Academic sort of
Skeptic, however, in that he combines ab-
stention from unconditional speculative
assent to transphenomenal realities with a
careful practical weighing of probable arguments, especially in regard to human
nature and morality. Hence he makes much
more generous drafts than does Montaigne
upon the moral teachings and even the
natural philosophy of his contemporaries,
the Christian Stoics. Their notions can be
used with some probability in learning
about man and developing the rules of
moral prudence in our individual and social spheres.

Thus Charronian human wisdom signifies the practical intellectual and moral
habit in the individual agent whereby he
remains always mindful of the need to
follow nature or divinely imparted reason
in realizing the ideal of self-control, con-
stancy, and contentment of mind. The humanly wise man is capable of

> regulating himself in all things according to nature, i.e., reason, the first and universal law and light inspired by God and which shines within us, to which he submits and conforms his own particular [reason]. . . . Therefore, here is the true plenary prudence (which is the foundation and pivot of virtue): to follow nature, i.e., reason.[11]

Whereas Montaigne interprets the imperative of following nature as meaning to be content with and enjoy our composite human being, Charron always equates it with accepting the judgment of a reason informed by the Stoic moral ideal and the Christian assurance about God as the source of reason and every natural norm.

By reference to nature as so interpreted, he can then deal more confidently with the postponed problem of specialized wisdoms and theological wisdoms. Taken in isolation, the former have only a technical significance of mastery and directive skill

11. *Ibid.*, Preface, p. 11; book II, chapter 3, p. 364.

within some particular area. But they can
be incorporated within the life of moral
agents who have integral prudence, thus
attaining a truly human meaning in the
service of the moral aims of individual and
social man. As for theological wisdom,
Charron treats it very circumspectly. It
consists actually of two sorts of wisdoms:
the strictly theological kind acquired
through study, and the gift received from
the Holy Spirit. He himself engages in
theological reasoning in other contexts,
but in his theory of wisdom he must accept the consequence of attacking all speculative demonstrative knowledge. Theological wisdom is therefore reinterpreted
to mean, not theological science, but a
certitude confined to faith itself and the
gift of wisdom. The man who shares in this
religious wisdom has the special duty of
acknowledging and supplementing the
human wisdom of the integrally prudent
man. The latter is naturally religious in
view of the requirements of justice toward
God, but his entire rectitude concerning
nature and reason is strengthened and

given a firm context by theological wisdom in this revised and contracted sense.

Charron intended his conception of moral-religious wisdom to provide men with something more morally demanding than Montaigne's joyful resignation to our mixed condition and something more definitely Christian than the natural religion of the early modern deists and freethinkers. He hailed human wisdom as the perfection of man as man, and moral philosophy in general as the great lamp for understanding man and ordering his conduct. But Charron's Skepticism left him quite exposed to the criticism of the freethinking Skeptics who did not accept the Christian faith. They asked why he chose one particular moral philosophy, namely, that of the Stoics as revised by Lipsius and Du Vair, and why he introduced large sections taken from moral theology. He did not furnish any definite ground for this direction of his moral thought, apart from its congeniality with his religious convictions and its probable strength in aiding the analysis of human actions.

The core difficulty between Charron
and the critics of his notion of wisdom as
plenary prudence concerned the unification of moral and religious wisdoms. He
argued that our religious office is an aspect of justice and hence that the really
wise man will combine plenary prudence
with religion. The latter is urged upon us
by moral wisdom itself.[12] But the freethinkers pointed out that this traditional reasoning supposed that we have some speculative knowledge of God and know with certainty about our real duty in justice to God,
a supposition which Charron was prevent-
ed from making except on probable
grounds. In order to defend the integration
of moral and religious wisdoms, Charron
had only two paths to follow. One was to
reaffirm the natural roots of wisdom in our
human desire for excellence of knowledge.
But he could not avail himself of the speculative development of the seeds of wisdom

12. *Ibid.*, II, 5, pp. 397-402. Charron's intended
     safeguard against the purely natural moral wis-
     dom of the freethinkers is not sufficiently weighed
     by E. F. Rice, *op. cit.*, pp. 179ff.

either in terms of specialized sciences
(which were morally neutral and could
not rectify the mind toward the full human good) or in terms of the philosophical
sciences (which fell under his own skeptical criticism of demonstrative knowledge).
Therefore, Charron was obliged to follow
the second path of invoking our faith in
revealed truths as the sole basis for the
conviction that the rule of nature is that
of a reason participating in the divine wisdom, and hence of a moral reason ordain-
ing the worship of God through religious
acts.

Within this perspective, the gift of wisdom does more than perfect and crown
man's natural human wisdom and piety:
it "authorizes" them in a much more radical sense than Charron likes to admit. A
religious wisdom grounded upon faith provides the ultimate and only certitudinal
backing for Charronian human wisdom,
and does so in such a way as to obscure
the wisdom of sacred theology and eliminate that of metaphysics. Moral and religious wisdom are brought together, but

only at the cost of isolating them from the speculative life of the intelligence in its philosophical and modern scientific forms. A wisdom of this sort does not delight to be with her many children but devours them, and then finds herself powerless to respond wisely to the challenges of man.

The Stoics and Skeptics of the Northern Renaissance made some valuable contributions to the theory of wisdom. They brought into new prominence some aspects of that theory which had been relatively neglected. The moral meaning for wisdom was sharply emphasized, and the distinction between the moral wisdom of the concrete agent and that leading to moral science was shown to be fraught with problems. Chief among these problems was whether moral wisdom in either sense required and could receive the support of speculative philosophy, whether the latter be understood as metaphysics or as a philosophy of nature including some doctrine on God. And at the other end of the scale, the question was raised whether moral wisdom in its scientific and prudential forms has any certitude and orientation apart from union with religious wisdom. The meanings of wisdom as sacred theology and as the gift of the Holy Spirit were quite sharply distinguished, usually to the disadvantage of the former and the widening of the latter's functions to include the underwriting of our natural wisdoms. Perhaps the growing specialization of labor was reflected in the interest also shown in the particularized types of wisdom and the need to rejoin them with the more comprehensive wisdoms of man.

None of these aspects of wisdom was truly novel, but belonged in the complex heritage received from Scripture and the Greek philosophers, the Fathers and the medieval theologians. But some of the emphases were new, especially the combination of moral and religious wisdom as a unit which tended to become self-sufficient. The characteristic tendency of the age was toward a disaggregation of the components in the medieval wisdom tradition. Although the intention was for achieving new sorts of unification among

several elements in that tradition, the actual result was to split them apart and to
weaken their distinctive significance. In a
word, the entire theory of wisdom and all
its constituents were clearly being subjected to a radical doubt by the early decades
of the seventeenth century.

This condition of uncertainty was
eventually reflected even in the Scholastic
textbooks of the period, despite their uniform citation of the common stock of defi-
nitions and divisions bearing on the Aristotelian theory of wisdom. The textbook authors could not agree about whether to
unify the philosophical theory of wisdom
around metaphysics, around a conjunction
of prudence and the moral virtues, or
around the popular idea of a formal system of principles regulating the whole
body of philosophical knowledge.[13] Nor

13.   A good contemporary report on the status of
      the question of wisdom among the seventeenth
      century manualists is given by Francisco de
      Oviedo, S.J., *Integer Cursus Philosophicus* (2
      vols.; Lyon: Prost, 1640). In the section on
      Logica, I, v, Oviedo lists as the three major mean-
      ings for wisdom: a collection of many sciences

did they seem to be aware of the full weight of the skeptical critique of our knowing powers and its adverse consequence for accepting any one of these centers of unification for human wisdom. Whether the conscientious pursuer of wisdom turned for guidance to the Skeptics, the Stoics, or the Scholastics at this time, he would soon discover that the foundations for one of the major goals of intellectual inquiry were thoroughly weakened and subjected to conflicting evaluations.

2. THE CARTESIAN THEORY OF WISDOM

It is sometimes imagined that Descartes' modernity consists in a firm repudiation of the ideal of wisdom, that he establishes his intellectual independence by refusing to agree with his medieval and Renaissance forbears that philosophy is

united in one man, an extraordinary excellence in some particular science or art, and the most perfect science in the Aristotelian sense of knowing from principles and through the most universal causes and as judging the principles of other sciences. (I, 62) The stress on principles is noteworthy.

really a search after wisdom. This seems to follow from his plan of renovating philosophy in accord with the same general sort of reasoning and certitude as is found in mathematics, a discipline which remains intrinsically distinct from metaphysical and moral wisdom. Descartes is thus treated as the very symbol of the radical displacement of wisdom by science within modern philosophy.

When we do him the honor of consulting his own writings, however, we are forced to take a quite different view of the role of wisdom in his thought. Whether we read Descartes' early annotations, his mature publications, or his intimate letters, we find him maintaining with remarkable consistency that genuine philosophy is indeed a study of wisdom and a pursuit of the wise way of living. This testimony cannot be regarded merely as a traditional echo remaining from his Jesuit education at La Flèche, and surviving either out of inadvertence or as a tactical means of conciliating his more tradition-minded friends. It is not simply an uncriticized element in

his mind, since he deliberately scrutinizes
the ideal of wisdom, submits it to the same
methodic tests as other prominent aspects
of his doctrine, and provides a formal theory about its nature and attainability. Nor
does Descartes play upon the note of wisdom merely as a way of predisposing people favorably toward his philosophy. He is
sufficiently aware of the intellectual situation in his own day to realize that handi-
caps as well as advantages attach to the
theme of wisdom. It takes a certain intellectual courage to accept the ideal of
wisdom at a time when it appears in the
school manuals as a tired and fruitless
topic, when the freethinkers seek to sub-
stitute philosophical wisdom for religious
faith, when the humanist interest in the
wisdom of the ancients makes the matter
seem remote and artificial, and when eso-
teric groups such as the Rosicrucians are
bringing ridicule upon the very notion of
wisdom by their inflated claims to hold its
secret. The problem of wisdom was too
controverted in Descartes' lifetime to permit its being used diplomatically as an easy

and guaranteed recommendation of his
own position.

When a philosopher becomes involved
in an intellectual crisis, he is likely to reveal to us the central axes of his own mind.
There are three revelatory crises in the life
of Descartes. The first occurs on that famous night in November of 1619, when he
has a series of dreams that open up the
prospect of a new and wonderful science
whose foundations he is called upon to
lay. The second crucial moment comes a
decade later, in 1628, when he sets down
on paper those rules for the mind's direction and those principles of metaphysics
out of which his entire philosophy is to
develop. And the third significant date is
1647, when Descartes seizes upon the oc-
casion of a French translation of his *Principles of Philosophy* to address himself
directly to ordinary readers of the vernacular and to influence people throughout
Europe.

Now, it is no mere coincidence that the
written record of Descartes' thoughts upon
each of these occasions manifests his deep

concern for the question of wisdom. At
these turning points spanning the thirty
years of his intellectual development, he
takes the trouble not just to mention wisdom but to treat it prominently as being
bound up most closely with his entire revo-
lution in philosophy. This pointed insistence means that his new conception of
philosophy entails a new conception of
wisdom, rather than an elimination of it
from the subjects of inquiry. Cartesian man
is not asked to abandon the ideal of human
wisdom but to revivify it or, more precisely
stated, to furnish himself for the first time
in intellectual history with the adequate
philosophical means of making it effective
in his reflections and practical life. This
prospect of realizing human wisdom under
pioneer conditions accounts for a certain
excitement attending Descartes' treatment
of philosophical method in these three instances. He is trying to convey to us that
any contribution he will make toward the
modern approach in philosophy will involve a strengthening of the human means
for attaining wisdom. The depth of his in-

volvement in the question of wisdom can
only be conveyed by analyzing in some detail the connection it has with these instructive situations.

Early thoughts on wisdom. In his third
and most fruitful dream at Ulm, Descartes
was confronted with two books: a dictionary from which he received little use and
an anthology of poems containing some
pregnant thoughts on truth, error, and
moral decision. As reported by his earliest
biographer, Descartes made a spontaneous
interpretation of his dream.

He judged that the *Dictionary* stood
merely for the sciences gathered together, and that the collection of
poems entitled *Corpus Poetarum*
marked more particularly and ex-
pressly the union of philosophy with
wisdom. For he did not think that we
should be so very much astonished to
see that poets, even those who but
trifle, abounded in utterances more
weighty, more full of meaning and
better expressed, than those found in
the writings of philosophers. He as-
cribed this marvel to the divine nature

of inspiration, to the might of phantasy, which strikes out the seeds of wisdom (existing in the minds of all men like sparks of fire in flints) far more easily and distinctly than does reason in the philosophers.[14]

This view of his dream fits in with all that we know about the young Descartes' outlook and, for our purposes, clearly testifies to the centrality of the theme of wisdom from the very start of his philosophical speculations.

The book of human learning had left Descartes profoundly dissatisfied with both the sciences and the philosophies of his time. The former were genuine instances of knowledge, but their unity was more of an extrinsic, dictionary sort than an organic and systematically justified

14. This is the account given in Abbe Baillet's *Life of M. Descartes*, trans. N. K. Smith, *New Studies in the Philosophy of Descartes* (London: Macmillan, 1952), p. 36. Baillet bases it upon Descartes' own *Cogitationes Privatae*, printed in the *Oeuvres de Descartes*, ed. C. Adam and P. Tannery (13 vols.; Paris: Cerf, 1897-1913), X, 217.

kind. As for the writings of professional philosophers, they struck Descartes as failing to supply that certitude, human urgency, and attractive presentation which we associate with a wise vision capable of organizing our knowledges and influencing our conduct. In a word, the burgeoning sciences lacked a philosophical basis for unification, whereas the books of philosophy lacked the depth and power of an effective wisdom. Anticipating Vico and Schelling and Heidegger, the young Descartes affirmed that there is more substantive wisdom in the poets than in those who ' call themselves philosophers. He could not discover wisdom anywhere present in a properly philosophical form, but this did not lead him to despair about realizing it. For he was convinced that the seeds of wisdom are latent in all minds and are given at least an imaginative embodiment in the works of the poets. The crucial question was whether the sparks of wisdom could also be fanned into a steady, visible flame by philosophical reason itself. Descartes was privately convinced that he had

a religious vocation to bring the meanings
of wisdom into a rational form which
would simultaneously constitute a philosophical knowledge, organize the sciences
into a single body, and guide our moral
choice to its proper end.

The reflections which occupied Descartes during the 1620's deepened his view
about the solidarity between his general
plan for philosophy and his effort to recon-
stitute wisdom in a philosophical form. The
first step in the latter direction was to
specify more carefully the origin of human wisdom, its goal and fulfillment, and
its characteristic use of imagery. Although
the surviving texts and comments on these
three points are of telegraphic brevity,
they are sufficiently informative to show
that the firm outlines of Descartes' mature
theory of wisdom were already taking
shape. Moreover, they were doing so within the context of a religious confidence that
the Lord God who is the creator of the
human mind is also the giver of wisdom,
even in the most relevant sense of giving
the intellectual strength to make the philo-

sophical analysis of the structure of wisdom.

Descartes places the origin of wisdom deep within the human spirit, in those connatural notions and meanings with which our spirit comes into existence from the creative power of God. Hence he refers to the seeds of science and wisdom, as well as to the sparks of wisdom buried in the flintstone of the human mind. These metaphors suggest that there is a vital predisposition in us all to enlarge our minds to the full condition of a wisdom knowledge. For men to desire and pursue wisdom is more basic than to seek the material conditions of life, since wise knowing and wise living are the core of our existence and not simply its condition.

Yet our human orientation in a general way toward the life of wisdom is prephilosophical and premethodic: it is fundamental but not assured of its own realization. The method and reasoning supplied by philosophy are like the tools needed to cultivate a precious seedling, like the summoning iron which arouses the light from

the flintstone and then brings it to steady
glow. A philosophical method which does
arouse and cultivate the fire of sapiental
intelligence is serving both the aim of our
own nature and the creative intention of
God. The Cartesian teaching on the native
thirst of men for wisdom is at once humanistic and theistic in its import.

In discussing the end toward which the
inclination to wisdom prompts us, Descartes keeps the metaphysical and moral
meanings for wisdom closely together. The
fullness of wisdom is to be found not solely
in comprehensive speculative knowledge
but also in moral understanding and control over conduct. Hence he is able to
speak synonymously about writing on wisdom and writing a treatise on *bona mens.*
This Stoic term plays a key role throughout
Descartes' various treatments of wisdom.
It is a reminder of his debt to the classical
and Renaissance Stoics for concentrating
upon contentment and moral sufficiency
of mind as being the wise man's aim. Re-
marking that "the sayings of the sages can
be reduced to some very small number of

general rules," Descartes makes good use
of the Stoic ethics.[15] It reinforces his own
emphasis upon the moral ingredient in
wisdom and also furnishes much of the
source material for his detailed account of
morality.

When Descartes opens the *Discourse
on Method* with the famous remark that
"good sense *[bon sens]* is mankind's most
equitably divided endowment," he is not
indulging in a fatuous optimism contra-
dicted by every sober survey of human history.[16] On the contrary, he is packing into
a single phrase the result of his early reflections on wisdom or *bona mens*. To attribute good sense to mankind is to attribute to it the seed of wisdom, considered in

15. *Loc. cit.* The role of wisdom in Descartes' early
     notations is brought out in the commentary by
     Henri Gouhier, *Les Premières pensées de Des-
     cartes* (Paris: Vrin, 1958), pp. 67-69, 79-85.
16. *Discourse on Method,* trans. L. J. Lafleur (New
     York: Liberal Arts Press, 1950), p. 1. For the
     relationship between *bon sens* and wisdom, in
     the very first sentence of the *Discourse,* read the
     commentary by E. Gilson, *René Descartes: Dis-
     cours de la méthode, texte et commentaire* (2d
     ed.; Paris: Vrin, 1939), pp. 81-83.

an initial and minimal way as an intellectual impulse toward gaining a masterful understanding of ourselves and our destiny.
Good sense is the basic germ of human
intelligence which is dynamically ordered
toward its proper perfection in speculative
and moral wisdom. Thus good sense and
bona mens are intrinsically and dynamically related as the initial and the terminal
moments in the human mind's quest of
wisdom. This immanent teleology of the
human spirit with respect to the possession
of wisdom survives the ban which Descartes eventually places upon teleological
explanation. Although that sort of explanation is excluded from the study of nature,
it is retained in full force for the interpretation of human reality. We only come
to self-understanding when we realize that
man is a wisdom-seeking being and that in
its possession lies the true end of human
existence.

There is also a definite link between
the Cartesian conception of wisdom and
the philosophical use of imagery. Reflect-
ing upon the fruitful use of symbols in

modern geometry, Descartes remarks that "just as the imagination employs figures to conceive bodies, so the intellect uses certain sensible bodies to figure forth spiritual realities, for instance, wind [and] light. Wherefore, in philosophizing on higher issues we can raise the mind in knowledge up to the summit."[17] Descartes says this, because of our human need for reassurance that we do have the intellectual resources to acquire wisdom and communicate it to others. We can take heart from the notable unification achieved in mathematics through the use of imaginative constructs, as well as from our capacity to provoke insight into spiritual realities through poetic imagery.

It is true that the pioneer mind of the philosopher must rely upon pure understanding rather than imagination in developing the method and system of philosophical wisdom. But for encouraging himself

17. *Cogitationes Privatae* (Adam-Tannery, X, 217). Francis Bacon and Vico were interested in the "wisdom of the ancients" found in classical mythology.

in this task, for expressing his findings, and
for persuading others to mount the same
path, he must learn how to fashion appropriate symbols and use telling images. Descartes' critique of imagination as a principal means for discovering philosophical
truth does not blind him to the human requirement of clothing the pursuit of wisdom in sensible form. Hence he himself
makes deliberate use of the image of the
master architect of the house of wisdom,
the systematic weaver of truth, the chain
of the sciences, and the tree of wisdom.
Once the imagination is removed from
supplying the basic criterion of evidence,
it can be used freely in other functions
within Cartesian philosophy, including
that of adapting the lofty ideal of wisdom
to the condition of the human composite.

Wisdom and the rules of method. By
1628, Descartes was confident about clos-
ing the gap between the latent seeds of
wisdom and the rational grasp upon speculative and moral truths in which a reflective philosophical wisdom consists. His
plan was to provide good sense with a uni-

versal method and a set of metaphysical
principles sufficiently powerful to yield the
embracing knowledge ideally attributed to
the wise man, but never before in human
history placed within our actual grasp. He
set down the methodological part of this
project in the *Rules for the Direction of
the Mind,* which even in its incomplete
manuscript form deeply impressed the philosophers of his century.

In order to save his readers from get-
ting bogged down in the details of methodology at the expense of seeing the goal
intended by his rules, Descartes made
pointed mention of wisdom in the very
first rule. The aim of intellectual endeavor
should be to obtain well evidenced, true
judgments about ourselves and God, the
natural world and human moral action.
But we cannot secure mastery of judgment in this comprehensive sense, if we
confine our attention to some specialized
field and think that it has no relations with
the other sciences and with the problem of
the unification of knowledge in an ordered
body. Expressed in another way, we can-

not really cultivate our minds apart from taking an active part in the search after wisdom.

> It seems especially remarkable to me that so many people should most diligently investigate the customs of men, the properties of plants, the motions of the heavens, the transmutations of metals, and the objects of similar disciplines, and at the same time give hardly a thought to proper thinking or to universal wisdom [*de bona mente, sive de hac universali Sapientia*], although all other subjects should be esteemed, not so much for themselves, as because they contribute something to this wisdom. . . . For all the sciences are nothing else but human wisdom, which always remains one and the same, however many different subjects it is applied to.[18]

Thus Descartes wanted anthropologists and biologists and chemists to feel that they have a vital stake in the quest for wis-

18. *Rules for the Direction of the Mind*, I, trans. L. J. Lafleur (Indianapolis: Bobbs-Merrill, 1961), pp. 3-4.

dom. As men who cultivate their intellect in a methodic way, they cannot help but have a radical need for a universal wisdom, as well as for the limited one found in their own specialty.

The Cartesian proposals on method are thus located firmly within the framework of that search after wisdom in speculative and practical matters in which everyone contributing to the intellectual life is somehow already engaged, perhaps without recognizing it. There is a close reciprocal relation between Descartes' theories on method and on wisdom, such that they mutually support and shape each other. This reciprocal influence is clearly detectable in respect to the unity of knowledge. On the mooted question of whether to identify human wisdom with some particular part of philosophy (such as metaphysics or ethics alone) or else with the interconnected body of sciences, Descartes accepts roughly the latter position. The notion of a unified whole of wisdom strengthens his view that there must be a single method with universal competence for determining the philosophical worth of all propositions and consolidating them into a single system of truths. At the same time, he uses his methodology to remove the vacuous, overinflated claims usually made by the Ramists and other partisans of a single system of the sciences. Cartesian wisdom is universal, not in the sense of an encyclopedic collection or a tabular diagram, but because it embodies a way of knowing through doubt-tested principles which can control the works of the mind in every area of inquiry. The unity of wisdom is not achieved by trying to eliminate the differences among the objects of the several sciences, but by analyzing the same pattern of intuition and deduction which Descartes regards as prevailing in every scientific investigation. Wisdom is one and universal, because it represents the full development of the common principles and method which yield firm judgments in every field.

One consequence of securing the unity of wisdom in close relation with his theory of method is that Descartes can settle the problem of science and wisdom in a non-skeptical fashion. He remains much closer on this issue to the Aristotelian tradition, which regards wisdom as the culmination of scientific knowing rather than as divorced from science, than he does to the Skeptics and many of the Stoics of his day. Since Descartes defends the human mind's ability to have true and certain knowledge about real beings, he cannot accept the skeptical limitation of wisdom to a purely personal prudence, filled out in some instances by a probabilist use of natural and moral philosophy. Instead, he defends the twofold statement that the act of scientific knowing can come within our grasp, but that it remains incomplete until it develops into an integral wisdom.

Cartesian wisdom draws the primary springs of its life, not from humanistic erudition and Stoic moral precepts, but emphatically from the same operations of intelligence which yield the well-grounded, certain judgments constituting knowledge in its scientific mode. To specify that philosophy is the study of wisdom is not to

assign to philosophy a purpose basically
different from the attainment of scientifically validated knowledge. It is only to
insist that the act of knowing be exercised
consistently and comprehensively, that the
common principles of human knowledge
be developed in all their systematic implications and unity, that the findings of special sciences be constantly assimilated to
this growing body of knowledge in the full
sense, and thus that the scientific resources
of man be worked out to their fruition in
human wisdom.

On this basis, Descartes is also prepared to eliminate the Renaissance dilem-
ma of choosing between a metaphysical
and a moral meaning for wisdom. Wisdom
is not found exclusively in either metaphysics or ethics, since its life consists precisely in the continuous movement of the
mind linking together all the interconnected truths in the various disciplines and
parts of philosophy. Within this totality of
human wisdom, metaphysics and ethics remain distinct. Each performs its own role
in building up the unity of human knowl-

edge, and these functional differences are
not wiped out. Yet there is no need to
choose between them as the real locus of
wisdom. Each shares in its own way in the
scientific character of judgment, and hence
each makes its own contribution to the
body of wisdom. The unity of wisdom is
essentially complex and includes both a
metaphysical and an ethical factor.

Within the context of the *Rules*, Descartes specifies an area of responsibility for
each factor.

> If someone takes for his problem the
> examination of all truths which hu-
> man reason is capable of knowing—
> which it seems to me should be done
> once in his life by everyone who seri-
> ously strives to develop wisdom—he
> will surely discover through the rules
> given that nothing can be known prior
> to the intellect itself, since the knowl-
> edge of all other things depends upon
> this, and not conversely.[19]

The man in search of wisdom cannot avoid
asking the radical question about the pri-

19.   *Ibid.*, VIII (Lafleur, p. 31).

mary truth and basis of certitude, and hence he cannot avoid engaging in metaphysical inquiry. Metaphysics concerns itself with such issues as the primary truth about the intellect and, in the process, secures the foundation for human wisdom as a whole. The principles of metaphysics are ultimately ordered, however, to the general requirements of wisdom and thus to the moral understanding of our life and its relation to God. Wisdom is not fully present until our mind has developed a moral philosophy which guides the will in the particular, contingent choices of human existence. In turn, moral teachings and particular moral decisions have the character of wisdom insofar as they draw upon the basic metaphysical truths.

Thus Descartes maintains a functional interdependence of metaphysics and ethics within the dominant context of wisdom. The wise man is he who grasps the primary truths about the Cogito, God, and the world in such fashion that he can then understand our composite nature, the contingencies of life, and the reference of human happiness to God. In a word, the wise man develops both metaphysical and ethical principles for the sake of achieving that firmness and certainty of judgment on speculative and practical matters in which the perfection of wisdom consists.

For twenty years after making his first sketch of the method and metaphysical principles of his philosophy, Descartes devoted himself to the task of elaborating his thoughts in a systematic order and thus filling in the content of his notion of philosophical wisdom. Then, a French translation of his *Principles of Philosophy* was completed in 1647, just three years before his death and just after he had succeeded in setting forth the main parts of his philosophy, with the notable exception of a moral philosophy. Descartes used this opportunity to issue a prefatory letter directing the attention of readers to the main features of his philosophy, especially the support it provides to pursuers of wisdom. There is a noticeable and understandable difference of tone in this treatment of wisdom by comparison with the earlier ones. Although his conception of wisdom remained basically unchanged, he could now refer to it in greater detail and with the confident knowledge of having actually elaborated most of the philosophical means for attaining it. Into a few highly concentrated pages, he compressed his working definition of wisdom, his procedure for dealing with a pluralism of wisdoms, his dominant image of the tree of philosophy, and some precisions on the moral and religious aspects of wisdom. To grasp Descartes' position on these topics is not only to approach the heart of his own philosophy but also to appreciate why the ideal of wisdom has continued to attract the major modern philosophers.

Definition of wisdom. Even after having developed his own philosophy in some systematic depth, Descartes refrains from making an outright identification of wisdom with philosophy. One reason for his reluctance to do so is his recognition that there are several kinds and degrees of wisdom and, consequently, that there is a special problem about the relationship of other kinds of wisdom with the philosophical wisdom in which he is primarily interested. Another consideration is that his own philosophy was not yet brought to completion and that he had some grounds for expecting further progress to be made by other men in the application of his principles. Hence even when he is explicitly treating of the philosophical kind of wisdom, Descartes preserves a certain distance between the ideal and the actuality. Along with the Stoics, he views philosophy as the study and search after wisdom, and refers to himself and every other genuine philosopher not as a possessor but as a student of wisdom, *studiosum sapientiae*. This is not a piece of conventional modesty but is entailed by his account of the nature of wisdom.

The reasoning behind Descartes' cautious position can be gathered from his working definition of wisdom.

By wisdom we not only understand prudence in affairs, but also a perfect knowledge of all things that man can know, both for the conduct of his life

and for the conservation of his health
and the invention of all the arts. . . .
It is really only God alone who has
perfect wisdom, that is to say, who
has a complete knowledge of the truth
of all things; but it may be said that
men have more wisdom or less according as they have more or less knowledge of the most important truths.[20]

This is a skillful analysis, since it begins
with our ordinary recognition of the restricted sort of wisdom displayed by the
man of practical skill, good management,
and prudent decision. Then, it directs us
toward the more proper meaning of wisdom as a perfect sort of knowledge and
hence as an intellectual perfection. There
is something outstanding and difficult
about this knowledge, however, because
of its universal range. Descartes is not say-

20.   *The Principles of Philosophy*, Preface, in *The
      Philosophical Works of Descartes*, trans. E. S.
      Haldane and G. R. Ross (2 vols.; corrected ed.;
      Cambridge: The University Press, 1931), I, pp.
      203-04. The sense in which Descartes' philosophy
      is a sustained essay in wisdom is determined by
      Joseph Combès, *Le Dessein de la sagesse car-
      tésienne* (Lyon-Paris: Vitte, 1960).

ing that knowledge at the high level of wisdom is solely practical in nature, but that it must be of such a sort as to yield certainty for determining the end of moral living and for the right use of the mechanical and medical knowledges of mankind.

He then introduces a distinction between the perfect condition of wisdom, which is found only in the divine mind, and the degrees of relative wisdom whereby men can approximate to God's embracing knowledge. This is not a trivial concession to tradition and piety on Descartes' part, since a number of important issues in his philosophy hinge upon recognizing that God has infinitely perfect knowledge and that all human knowledge involves some limitations. Spinoza makes us aware of how crucial this distinction between divine and human wisdoms really is, since he notes how it underlies the Cartesian position on error and certainty, divine freedom and human contentment of mind. If the fulness of wisdom is present in God, then we have assurance that His creative act and providential governance are wise and well ordered. We can also have confidence in the inferential use of our mind according to a philosophical method which promises to make us masters over our own passions.

Perfect wisdom, which is an actuality in respect to God, remains an ideal for men to strive after. What they can actually attain through the Cartesian philosophy is a reliable knowledge of the fundamental truths about oneself and God, nature and practical living. That is why Descartes lays such great stress upon a certitudinal knowledge of fruitful principles. His philosophy serves the cause of wisdom by furnishing us with the method, the primary principles, and the right order of reasoning for securing this basic knowledge and orienting us in the direction of plenary wisdom. Thus wisdom is an ideal, not in the depleting sense of a standard which we cannot ever hope to match, but in the humanly encouraging sense of a knowledge which we can fundamentally possess and yet always deepen and expand. And philosophy is called the study of wisdom to convey this twofold meaning of sure attainment and constant pursuit, evidential grasp upon principles and energetic cultivation of them for their human implications. Because it serves these two functions, Descartes recommends his philosophy as the most reliable path to human wisdom.

Into his general description of wisdom, he is also careful to introduce a note of obligation, so that the ideal will be regarded as a demanding one for a reflective human being. "Men, in whom the principal part is the mind, ought to make their principal care the search after wisdom, which is its true source of nutriment."[21] Man is a caring being, and it is Descartes' contention that human concern should be directed not primarily toward death but toward the pursuit of wisdom. To orient our life in this way is both to affirm the primacy of mind in our own nature and also to acknowledge the duty of feeding our mind upon the most significant sort of knowl-

21. *Principles of Philosophy*, Preface (Haldane-Ross, I, 205).

edge. In proposing wisdom as the common ideal for men, Descartes is prolonging the Renaissance drive toward despecializing the general meaning of wisdom, toward making it available to people other than the professional philosophers and theologians. However, he widens out the appeal of wisdom not by making it any the less speculative and philosophical but precisely by associating wisdom with his own philosophy, which is designed for being apprehended by any person of reflective capacity. There is something obligatory about the ideal of human wisdom, because man the minded being has the resources for placing himself in fundamental possession of the philosophical method and principles leading to a knowledge in the mode of wisdom.

The degrees of wisdom. At this point, Descartes anticipates that we may make a calm comparison between his rather exalted view of our vocation to seek wisdom and the actual condition of human thinking, and then conclude that there is an unbridgeable gap between the two. He admits the fact of the discrepancy, and then takes great pains to uncover its sources and reduce its distance.

Although we have a minimal awareness that our minds are made for truth, we become easily discouraged about ever attaining it in the extraordinary degree required by wisdom. One reason for this discouragement stems from the failure of our informal attempts at settling the major issues affecting our existence. But Descartes suggests that this experience of failure should induce us to infer, not that the human mind is radically beyond its depth in general questions, but rather than it cannot handle them apart from a proper method and order of investigation.

A second source of discouragement comes, however, from the very authorities whom we consult in philosophy on the nature of man and his relation with God and the world. After giving our initial trust to the philosophers, we find them disagreeing violently among themselves over these issues and reaching conclusions which do not seem befitting for a wise man to hold.

We are apt to conclude that, if this be the outcome of the search after wisdom on the part of those best equipped to engage in it, then there is no likelihood that ordinary minds can make any headway. Here, Descartes readily admits that those who are called philosophers often do propose teachings and lines of conduct which strike us as being singularly unwise. Instead of accepting the skeptical conclusion, however, he observes that this criticism implicitly allows that we can discern sound from faulty reasoning on at least some basic matters touching on our nature and moral duty. There are some available criteria for judging the claims of writers to be our guides on the road to wisdom, and hence we need not despair of attaining some measure of wisdom.

But the decisive consideration for showing that wisdom is a workable human ideal lies in the plural condition of actual human wisdoms. We are not really in the position of having to choose between a perfect knowledge of all humanly relevant matters and no human wisdom what-

soever. Human wisdom is not only distinct
from divine wisdom (although they are
not unrelated) but is also internally dif-
ferentiated into several modes and degrees.
There are several kinds of human wisdom,
and no man is so alienated from the human condition as to be a stranger to one
or another of the forms of wisdom. The
search for wisdom is a gradual affair involving a normal growth on the part of the
human mind, as it learns how to use, criticize, and integrate the several modes of
human wisdom.

Descartes makes his most original contribution to the theory of wisdom in treating the problem of pluralism of human
wisdoms. There is a text which offers a
synoptic view of his doctrine on this pluralism and which must therefore be given
here, despite its length.

> I should here have succinctly ex-
> plained in what all the knowledge we
> now possess consists, and to what de-
> grees of wisdom we have attained.
> The first of these contains only no-
> tions which are of themselves so clear

that they may be acquired without any meditation. The second comprehends all that which the experience of the senses shows us. The third, what the conversation of other men teaches us. And for the fourth we may add to this the reading, not of all books, but especially of those which have been written by persons who are capable of conveying good instruction to us, for this is a species of conversation held with their authors. And it seems to me that all the wisdom that we usually possess is acquired by these four means only; for I do not place divine revelation in the same rank, because it does not lead us by degrees, but raises us at a stroke to an infallible belief. There have indeed from all time been great men who have tried to find a fifth road by which to arrive at wisdom, incomparably more elevated and assured than these other four. That road is to seek out the first causes and the true principles from which reasons may be deduced for all that which we are capable of knowing; and it is those who have made this their special work who have been called philosophers. At the same time I do not know that up to the present day there have been any in whose case this plan has succeeded. ... The true principles by which we may arrive at that highest point of wisdom in which the sovereign good of the life of man consists, are those which I have put forward.[22]

The immediate purpose of this passage is to remove the difficulty previously mentioned of the discouraging interval between the desire for wisdom and the actual results achieved even by those who call themselves lovers of wisdom. Descartes' reply is to suggest that we approach to wisdom by those gradual steps which do lie within our power, and that we do not permit ourselves to be distracted by philosophical essays which were really prephilosophical in the sense of not using the

22. *Ibid.* (Haldane-Ross, I, 205-06, 208). J. Segond, *La Sagesse cartésienne et la doctrine de la science* (Paris: Vrin, 1932), pp. 49-62, explains this text as a progressive dialectic of the five degrees of wisdom. My own reading of it employs a principle of continuity and discontinuity, especially between the first four degrees and the fifth or philosophical degree of wisdom.

method and principles developed by himself.

It will repay us to analyze carefully each of the degrees of wisdom mentioned in this text by Descartes. Before doing so, however, it is worth noting that he employs such terms as "roads," "methods," and "degrees" (or "grades"), all of which suggest our making a gradual approach to wisdom. Although he usually uses these terms synonymously, we can make a useful distinction among them. The word "roads" suggests the relative independence of one way to wisdom in respect to the others, and especially conveys the fact that a man may be familiar with some of them and not with the others. A "method" of wisdom signifies some particular road to wisdom considered insofar as we reflect upon its nature and employ its resources in a deliberate, systematic way. But do all the roads and methods lead eventually to the one same human wisdom? Descartes is prepared to give a highly qualified affirmative answer to this question, and for that purpose he refers to the "degrees" of wisdom. This term suggests both that we should make a gradual exploration of the riches of wisdom and that we should incorporate the lesser modes of wisdom into the definitive context of Cartesian philosophical wisdom. By reference to the latter standard, the other conceptions of wisdom are lesser degrees, but they invariably contain some sound elements which must be contributed to the plenary philosophical wisdom.

That Descartes does not intend any abandonment of the lower degrees of wisdom is clearly seen in his account of the first type of wisdom. It consists of those clear, but not fully distinct, deliverances of good sense which we have even apart from reflective meditation and methodic inference. The natural vigor of our intelligence enables us to ascertain the basic significance of the human acts of thinking and perceiving, imagining and willing, as well as the import of unity and certainty. In a certain sense, these simply apprehended meanings must be counted among the principles of human knowledge, since

they are involved in all our inquiries and
always impel us to probe further into their
implications. It is their inciting function
to keep the human mind dissatisfied with
its particular findings and its restricted
forms of wisdom or skill, and thus to keep
open a pathway toward a comprehensive
kind of human wisdom. Under the head-
ing of this first degree of wisdom, Descartes includes his earlier doctrine on the
seed-and-tree relationship between good
sense and *bona mens*. Since we all share
in the first grade of wisdom on the strength
of our having a human intelligence, we
also share in the dynamic tendency of that
intelligence to move toward wisdom or
proper thinking in the most inclusive sense.

Clearly, it is not to Descartes' advantage to counsel that we leave behind this
first degree of wisdom, as we might leave
behind us the first rung on a ladder or the
first turn on a road. The wide distribution
of a good sense which also turns out to be
a germinal wisdom assures him of the
widespread appeal of his ideal for human
inquiry. When he appeals over the heads

of the schoolmen to everyman as a thinking being, he does so in the very definite
sense of appealing to the germinal wisdom
of the first degree and its teleological ordination toward the philosophical wisdom
embodied in his system. In this theory of
the initial step of wisdom also lies the
source of Descartes' confidence that there
is no radical opposition between science
and wisdom, whether "science" be taken
in the Aristotelian or the modern sense.
The various sciences and branches of philosophy are developed under the impetus
received from the primary notions of good
sense. Just as there is unity in the source
of scientific and philosophic specialization,
so is there unity in the terminus of wisdom
toward which all our intellectual works
are convergently moving.

Nevertheless, Descartes imposes a serious restriction upon the first degree of
wisdom, as a reminder that the active germ
is not yet the fully grown organism. The
primary notions of our mind are valid as
directly presented meanings, but they carry
with them no warrant concerning the ex-

istential order. Their validity is confined to
the meanings themselves, without author-
izing any inferences about real things.
The meanings are clear enough to arouse
our intellectual wonder and research, but
they are not distinct enough, or tested ade-
quately by doubt concerning their existential status, to yield truths about existent
human beings. Hence, the primary notions
of good sense are not the unqualified first
principles of knowledge, and do not dis-
pense us from using a philosophic method
and elaborating a body of wisdom in the
mode of philosophical knowledge.

This limitation placed upon the first
degree of wisdom permits us to understand how Descartes handles the objection
that his method of doubt either strips the
mind so bare that it cannot even recognize
the meaning of the proposition about the
Cogito or else relies upon some already
valid notions and hence is superfluous.
The method of doubt is not intended to
eliminate the primary deliverances of good
sense, precisely because they are confined
to notional meanings and determine noth-

ing by themselves about existential truths. These meanings remain intact and fully operative even in the methodically suspensive mind, so that the statement about the Cogito is meaningful. It is not only meaningful, however, but also big with the mind's intent of seeking wisdom in its philosophically intensive sense. Hence Descartes does not fear that methodic doubt will destroy our native love of philosophical wisdom: rather, it furnishes the necessary condition so that this inclination can be soundly grounded in the existential, certain principles which will yield the desired comprehensive knowledge.

In view of the severe criticism of the senses enjoined by the method of doubt, it is somewhat disconcerting to find sense experience listed by Descartes as the second degree of wisdom. How can the senses contribute anything positive toward wisdom and still merit the strictures of his method? For a satisfactory answer, we must consider closely the way in which Descartes uses the term "senses" within the context of the theory of methodic doubt. By that term, he means there the "judgments formed without consideration in childhood."[23] He subjects them to doubt on the ground that such judgments were made precipitately before we had the full use of reason, and therefore were obstacles to a mature consideration of the truth. Thus the precise target of Cartesian doubt in this area is not the physiological states of the body and not even the perceiving act, regarded simply as attending to such states. What must be doubted are the judgments we make on the basis of our sensations, feelings, and appetites.

Even this is not expressed with sufficient accuracy, however, since not everything about sense-based judgments is germane to the technique of doubt. What Descartes counsels us to treat initially as false are two matters of content and three matters of circumstance associated with such judgments. The points of content are the assertion of extramental existence made

---

23.   *Principles of Philosophy*, I, 76 (Haldane-Ross, I, 253); cf. *ibid.*, I, 1 (Haldane-Ross, I, 219).

about the objects of sensation and the further assertion that these objects resemble in all respects their sensible representations. The circumstantial traits are that these judgments of existence and resemblance are made in haste and without methodic caution, are treated as primary sources of knowledge of real existents, and are soon hardened into powerful but undetected prejudices shaping our entire view of the real. It is this complex of meaningful qualifications which is stenographically compressed into the methodic precept that we should doubt the senses.

We may still wonder whether anything about sense-based judgments remains after doubt, even as so qualified, has withdrawn the assent of the methodic mind. Descartes' affirmative reply is his way of clarifying the second step along the way to wisdom. There remain at least the *cogitationes*, the acts of consciousness themselves, namely, the sensations and feelings and appetites. They have a certain intrinsic structure or formal being which can be analyzed and affirmed in judgments remaining valid throughout the entire investigation. Descriptive judgments reporting on the properties of our conscious acts and the pragmatic values contained therein are permanently valid meanings and, as such, are not revoked by methodic doubt. Taken by themselves, these meanings supply no warrant in Cartesian perspective for making any intellectual commitment about the existence and nature of anything distinct from our own acts of mind. Nevertheless, they do furnish some significant and indispensable questions for methodical inquiry. In this respect, there is a likeness and continuity between the primary notions of good sense and this salvageable core of sense-grounded judgments. Without some permanent orientation from the latter sort of experiences and feelings, we could not develop our belief in a real and valuable material world and in human nature as a composite reality. Descartes is obliged to follow a very involuted path for justifying this belief, but it does serve to give direction and relevance to his whole inquiry and hence it does contribute permanently toward the search after wisdom.

Nevertheless, in the concrete, our sensory judgments are not neatly dissected into the restricted but permanent core and the aspects of content and circumstance which are vulnerable to methodic doubt. All these aspects are fused and confused in our actual attitude toward a world of sensible things. We ordinarily fail to reflect upon the different epistemological status of these components, to separate one strand from the other, and to confine our initial assent to the descriptive minimum about the acts of our own awareness. For Descartes, this means that in its pre-philosophical condition, the wisdom of the senses is not disentangled from error, and is not in a sufficiently clear and distinct condition to provide a solid basis for the mind's odyssey toward wisdom. Judgments founded upon sensations and feelings are not yet clearly sifted, are not set off firmly from their extramental existential reference, and not yet reduced to a subsequent place in the order of philosophical reasoning which does bear upon existential questions.

Our present purpose is not to criticize Descartes on this fundamental issue for a realistic philosophy, but rather to understand how he can simultaneously designate sense-derived knowledge as the second degree of wisdom and also mount a strong attack upon the senses as primary sources of existential and metaphysically foundational knowledge. He does so by distinguishing between the initial deliverances of the senses leading to judgments about our own states of awareness, and the as yet untested judgments we are then inclined to make about beings distinct from our own mind. Once the methodic doubt is brought into play, Descartes will liberate the first function of judgment from the second, and thus will provide a safe way of using the testimony of sensation and feeling for purposes of philosophical wisdom. When this testimony is deprived of primary significance for being, it can be utilized not only for internal descriptions but also for determining subsequent questions about the actual course of nature and the arrangement of things which best serve human needs. The content of human wisdom can thus be enriched by the senses, once the necessary steps of method are taken and the proper order of philosophical reasons followed.

One aspect of Cartesian wisdom which comes to the fore at this point is the role of the will. In order to achieve a rigid restriction of the sensory kind of evidence, Descartes distinguishes between the perception of meanings by the intellect and the judgmental act of assent on the will's part. For advancing the development of wisdom, it is not enough to have meanings presented for pure intellection: the will must also critically respond to the meanings considered precisely as existentially evidenced and true. The ordering of truths in a systematic body of wisdom cannot be achieved solely through analysis of meanings, but requires reflective judgment on the existential bearing of these meanings and hence requires the controlled operation of judgmental will. Descartes proposes to base wisdom upon some existential truths about self, God, and world which the understanding perceives and the will assents to in true judgment. Hence he includes a practical as well as a speculative component in the fabric of wisdom, right from the very start of his philosophy. This is his long-range safeguard so that no deep clefts will open up between the metaphysical, ethical, and prudential moments in the growth of human wisdom. A man can become truly wise only when he philosophizes with both his intellect and his will —the Cartesian equivalent of Plato's maxim that we should philosophize with our whole soul.

We can conveniently treat the third and fourth degrees of wisdom together, since they concern two modes of receiving wise instructions from other people. The sources of human wisdom are not purely introspective, for the reflective person is aided by his education, his conversations, and his reading. Social intercourse and books therefore make their distinctive contribution to the wisdom tradition. Another paradox seems to be in the making, however, when this aspect of Descartes' theory of wisdom is compared with some of his other positions. It is difficult to reconcile his recognition of social channels of wisdom with his strongly stated distrust of erudition and the sanction of history, philosophical schools and their authority, as well as with his reduction of the starting point of philosophy to the individual thinking self. The social grades of wisdom do not sit comfortably alongside of the Cartesian image of the single master architect who reconstructs the city of philosophy and wisdom from cleared ground.

Nevertheless, Descartes does not criticize intellectual history or specify the Cogito situation in such a fashion as to rule out all the social sources of wisdom. It is true that he does propose the ideal of the autarchic thinker finding the first principle and rule of philosophical truth within himself, and does recommend self-instruction as the only sure path of philosophizing. Yet he places some qualifications upon these positions precisely so that he can

have a way of taking advantage of the social sources of wisdom. There are two
pertinent sets of distinctions applicable
here: that between the meanings furnished
by society and history and their tested interpretation in philosophical judgment,
and that between Descartes' own peculiar
function and that of subsequent minds
agreeing with his principles.

As far as his own life was concerned,
Descartes was indebted to his teachers at
La Flèche, to Mersenne and a wide com-
pany of other correspondents, and to the
ordinary people whom he observed in
many lands. He profited immensely from
his study of the great book of the world of
his own contemporaries and also from the
great book of past authors. Admittedly, he
drew many hints for his method or the logic
of philosophical wisdom from observing
the course of spoken discussions, from
reading the treatises of the Greek mathe-
maticians, and from classroom instruction
received in Scholastic logic. And in terms
of content, his conception of wisdom contained many resonances originating from

the Platonic and Aristotelian traditions on wisdom, perhaps as they were gathered together by the Coimbra Jesuit commentators. Especially for the moral dimensions of wisdom, Descartes also made generous drafts upon the Stoic and Skeptical sources current in his day. Hence in acknowledging the social aspects of wisdom, he was doing no more than justice to the men from whose living conversation and writings he learned so much.

Yet Descartes tried to learn from these social sources in a distinctive way. From conversation and reading, he drew hints of meaning which then had to be tested for their evidential worth, systematic role, and corrected philosophical significance. For instance, the Aristotelian definition of wisdom as universal knowledge through the highest causes and principles provided him with a definite direction of research concerning the knowledge-character of wisdom. But it remained a purely formal framework, until he could establish to his own satisfaction that he had the distinctive principles which would actually yield such knowledge and thus yield wisdom. Again, the Cartesian ideal of wisdom was definitely colored by the Stoic insistence upon integral prudence and contentment of mind. Descartes would have needlessly impoverished his study of wisdom, had he tried to ignore or deny this influence. Still, he was bound to inquire whether moral wisdom has any basis in metaphysics and whether the wise man can really attain to stability apart from any philosophically established reference to God.

By systematically subjecting all social sources of instruction to the method of doubt and the ordering of his philosophical inferences, Descartes sought to separate the socially communicated meaning itself from any claims recommending its acceptance on the ground of its being age-old, widely accepted, or already philosophical in nature. His policy was to distinguish between a social origin for some meanings of wisdom and a socially grounded basis of authority for accepting them as philosophically sound. Once the social channels brought a meaning of wisdom to his atten-

tion, he then made it take its own chances
of winning his assent on the strength of
the evidence discovered for it within his
own methodic context. Thus Descartes
could treat social intercourse and intellectual tradition as degrees of wisdom,
without diminishing his bar upon using
these sources as the motives of assent to
propositions concerning wisdom. To Descartes as well as to any other human intelligence, wisdom came in a social context,
but one which he regarded as constituting
a prephilosophical proposal of meaning
(even in the case of philosophical sources
of doctrine on wisdom) and not as an already certified portion of true wisdom.

Descartes agrees with Aristotle that one
mark of the wise man is his ability to communicate his own doctrine. The wise man
cannot simply rely upon the minimal good
sense in all men to catch his teaching; he
must work skillfully to present the grounds
of wisdom and make it compellingly attractive for other minds. He must use
imagery as well as argument in the communication of his wisdom to others. This

is the other social dimension in the problem of wisdom. Not only is Descartes open to discussion and reading for the formation of his notion of wisdom, but he recognizes the duty of reinserting his own teaching on the topic into the social media of schools and books. Whether he is addressing his Jesuit teachers or the Doctors of the Sorbonne, Hobbes or the Princess Elizabeth, he asks them to treat his remarks on wisdom as proposals which in turn must be verified by their own minds. Even when there is question of teaching the definitive Cartesian wisdom, its social mode of communication does not permit any substitution of extrinsic considerations for a personal seeing of its principles of evidence. The social mode of wisdom has to remain instrumental for Cartesians as well as for Descartes, even though their reflective assent makes them collaborators with him in completing the edifice of wisdom laid out according to his master plan.

In the central text around which the present comment on the degrees of wisdom is organized, it will be noticed that

Descartes does not proceed immediately from the fourth to the culminating fifth degree of wisdom, which is philosophy proper. Instead, he interrupts his analysis at this point of transition in order to state explicitly that religious wisdom is not included among the grades of human wisdom under discussion. One purpose for this move is to reserve religious wisdom for separate consideration, and we will follow Descartes' example here by postponing the problem of religious wisdom. But there are two immediate advantages for his direct exposition of the types of human wisdom. The interruption enables him to group together the first four degrees of wisdom in a definite unity, and then it helps him to bring out more effectively the distinctive nature of philosophical knowledge as the fifth sort of wisdom.

The first four modes of wisdom agree in part being only partial views of it. Yet they are not even constitutive parts, in the way that individual mosaic pieces are parts which can be joined together in an order to comprise the whole picture. These four degrees do not add up to the entire human meaning of wisdom, even when they are united. In conjunction as well as singly, they remain incomplete accounts of wisdom which fail to supply the proper philosophical foundation for it. They remain radically prephilosophical, in the sense of conveying meanings of wisdom which still have to be tested for their evidence and limits. Hence, Descartes can readily admit his debt to these preliminary ways to wisdom, without fearing that this will compromise in any degree his standards for rigorous knowledge as applied to the wisdom level of knowledge.

Nonetheless, he realizes that there is a certain danger latent in his admission of several grades and methods of wisdom, namely, that it will encourage some people to absolutize a particular one as self-sufficient. When this happens, there is a rapid change from ways of wisdom into blind alleys on the part of the already enumerated degrees. As a careful reader of Montaigne and Francis Bacon, it does not escape Descartes' notice that the sources of wisdom and those of folly and error are closely intertwined in the human mind. Hence we can make an instructive correlation between the first four Cartesian degrees of wisdom and the Baconian idols of the mind.

There is only a hairsbreadth separating the primary notions or first seeds of Cartesian wisdom from the Baconian idol of the tribe, the group of misconceptions arising out of the common structure of the human mind. A similarly narrow borderline separates the second sort of wisdom based upon meanings given in sensation and feeling and the idol of the cave, which stands for the peculiar prejudices coming from our private life. And finally, Bacon's idols of the marketplace and the philosophical forum are cautionary signs of the pitfalls lying in wait for anyone who absolutizes the mode of wisdom drawn from social intercourse and the study of philosophical traditions. Descartes is treading a perilous path, then, when he explores the lower degrees of wisdom, since they are easily transformed into countermethods and terminal wisdoms hostile to Cartesian philosophical wisdom itself. This requires him to be careful about establishing the nature of the transition needed from the earlier degrees of wisdom to the philosophical mode of wisdom.

He meets this challenge by using what I will call *the continuity-discontinuity principle*. There is both continuity and discontinuity between the first four steps toward wisdom and the fifth degree or Cartesian philosophical wisdom. There is continuity, not because the lesser forms of wisdom generate the higher through some intrinsic dialectic, but because they are avenues furnishing some meanings used in the final philosophical reconstruction of wisdom. These meanings become incorporated into philosophical wisdom only by submitting to the conditions laid down quite independently by the Cartesian methodology and systematic structure themselves. What makes the previously described types of wisdom preliminary or lesser degrees is precisely the transformation which they must undergo before being accepted as components in a reflective philosophical conception of wisdom. Thus there is also a definite discontinuity involved: it concerns the mode of knowledge even more than the content of meaning contributed to the conception of wisdom. The particular fragment of meaning for wisdom drawn from one of the first four sources must be methodically tested, reinterpreted by the Cartesian criterion of truth, and reordered according to the philosophical sequence of thoughts.

This interplay between a continuous and a discontinuous relationship among the preliminary and the definitive modes of wisdom helps to illumine Descartes' position on the history of philosophy. He does not share the obscurantist attitude toward learning and philosophical traditions on wisdom. Of Plato and Aristotle he remarks that "these two men had great minds and much wisdom acquired by the four methods mentioned before."[24] He makes similar acknowledgments about other great think-

24. *Ibid.*, Preface (Haldane-Ross, I, 206).

ers. But in all instances, he specifies that their wisdom was acquired by the first four methods, that it could not rise above the level of these sources, and consequently that there was still room for major work in the theory of wisdom. Indeed, Descartes is maintaining that the great sources in the wisdom tradition are using methods of knowledge which can only yield what he regards as a prephilosophical kind of wisdom. He is the fountainhead for a long line of modern philosophers who think that previous speculation on wisdom furnishes only the materials for philosophical knowledge and not wisdom itself in the philosophical mode. Like Hegel and Nietzsche and Heidegger, he suggests that the history of philosophical wisdom is constituted by himself and begins properly with his own theory of wisdom. These thinkers confuse incisive criticism with a reduction of previous speculation to the status of a prehistory for their special theory of wisdom.

It is this exaggerated use of the continuity-discontinuity principle which underlies the following amazing claim made

by Descartes for his doctrine of philosophical wisdom.

> Although all the truths which I place
> in my *Principles* have been known
> from all time and by all men, never-
> theless there has never yet been any
> one, as far as I know, who has recog-
> nized them as the principles of philos-
> ophy, that is to say, as principles from
> which may be derived a knowledge
> of all things that are in the world [and
> hence a philosophical kind of wis-
> dom].[25]

The first part of this statement rests upon
his conviction about the measure of good
sense and germinal seeds of wisdom de-
posited in all men. But as long as our speculations remain in the untutored condition
of a mind not yet disciplined by his own
method of doubt, Descartes is unwilling
to regard the results as really transcending

25. *Ibid.*, Preface (Haldane-Ross, I, 209). That
    human wisdom is a limited but orderly develop-
    ment of content and reasons from recognized
    principles of knowledge is the keynote of M.
    Guéroult's *Descartes selon l'ordre des raisons* (2
    vols.; Paris: Aubier, 1953), I, pp. 18-20.

"the common and imperfect knowledge
[la connaissance vulgaire et imparfaite]
which may be acquired by the four methods" or inferior grades of wisdom.[26] Truths
are present in this infraphilosophical type
of knowledge which characterizes the doctrine of even his philosophical predeces-
sors, but they are not grasped in a way that
will issue in philosophical wisdom. For
Descartes, the passage from the lower to
the highest form of knowledge takes place
through an act of intellectual recognition.
The philosopher is the one who learns to
recognize the common human truths and

26. *Principles of Philosophy,* Preface (Haldane-
     Ross, I, 210). This enables us to give a more
     precise meaning to the word "common" (*vulgaris*)
     in such a text as *ibid.,* IV, 200 (Haldane-Ross,
     I, 296), where Descartes maintains: "I have
     nevertheless made use of no principle which has
     not been approved by Aristotle and by all the
     other philosophers of every time; so that this
     philosophy [of mine], instead of being new, is
     the most ancient and common of all." Cartesian
     philosophy is common, as incorporating the seeds
     of wisdom, but is not common in the sense of
     remaining at the infraphilosophical level of spec-
     ulation lacking in intuitive-deductive systematic
     principles.

meanings for wisdom precisely as the principles of an entire philosophical system.
He sees for the first time their significance
and function as principles of deduction for
the full order of philosophical truths. It is
his recognition of the truths about self,
God, and the world precisely as constituting the principles of deductive explanation
for the whole system which brings these
truths from the nonphilosophical to the
philosophical manner of wisdom.

Even so, we may be inclined to ask, is
not this a repetition of the merest commonplace in the textbooks about metaphysical
wisdom as being the universal knowledge
of the highest causes and principles? In
reply, Descartes appeals to the distinction
between principles of being and principles
of knowledge. What he regards as unique
in his philosophy is that it admits to the
role of principles only those truths (whether they concern knowing or being) which
can function precisely as principles of
knowledge in the deduction of a full system of explanation. Hence, by definition,
he confines the act of intellectual recogni-

tion constitutive of philosophical wisdom
to the act of grasping those doubt-resistant
and system-yielding truths whose causal
efficacy lies in the noetic order or in the
realm of producing a tightly forged chain
of certain reasons. Only after the lower degrees of wisdom are surveyed from this
new perspective can their meanings be
incorporated into the body of wisdom in
its formally philosophical perfection.

Descartes' response is not entirely satisfactory. It does establish a proportion between the kind of systematic knowledge he
is seeking and the kind of recognition he
requires for philosophical principles. There
is general agreement among philosophers
that the transition from nonphilosophical
to philosophical knowledge requires a reflective act of recognition. But that act
need not be specified toward the particular
sort of intuitive-deductive system of reasoning envisaged by Descartes. Wherever
there is criticism of the Cartesian conception of knowledge, there will also be dis-
agreement with him over the kind of principles needed to arrive at philosophical

wisdom. If metaphysics is viewed as rest-
ing upon principles of being as well as
those of knowing, then this is bound to
lead to another explanation of the nature
of wisdom-yielding principles and the act
of recognizing them. Thus Descartes makes
an overclaim at this point, when he regards
all previous doctrines on wisdom as prephilosophical and reserves philosophical
wisdom exclusively for his own account of
the relationship between noetic principles
and their systematic consequences.

The tree of philosophical wisdom. In
order to understand Descartes' position on
moral and religious wisdom, we must first
of all grasp the connection between his
theory of wisdom and his famous simile
of the tree of philosophy.

> Philosophy as a whole is like a tree
> whose roots are metaphysics, whose
> trunk is physics, and whose branches,
> which issue from this trunk, are all
> the other sciences. These reduce
> themselves to three principal ones,
> viz. medicine, mechanics and morals
> —I mean the highest and most perfect
> moral science which, presupposing a

complete knowledge of the other sciences, is the last degree of wisdom.[27]

Although wisdom in the unqualified sense
is not identical with philosophy, still it is
true for Descartes that the divisions of
philosophy are nothing other than the ar-
ticulations of wisdom in its most developed natural form. The organic image of
the tree of philosophical wisdom helps to
convey the continuity of the reasoning and
the fruitfulness of the principles which constitute the body of philosophy. It also
helps us to resolve some questions usually
asked about the order and rooting of Cartesian philosophy.

Cartesian order is governed by the
functional relationship among propositions
established through the acts of intuition
and deduction and their supplementary
operations. It is not appropriate to ask,
therefore, whether the metaphysics is there
for the sake of the physics, or the latter for
the sake of the ethics. Within the context
of the tree of philosophical wisdom, no
one of these parts is intended unilaterally

27.   *Ibid.*, Preface (Haldane-Ross, I, 211).

for the sake of another one, but all are given a finality in respect to the unity of philosophical wisdom as a single body. The latter furnishes the governing principle for the order and functions of the parts of philosophy. Instead of pitting Descartes the metaphysician against Descartes the natural philosopher or the moralist, we are taught by the image of the philosophical tree to organize all these aspects of his work around the main task of cultivating the sapiential ideal.

We are familiar today with Martin Heidegger's striking question (derived from Husserl) concerning the Cartesian tree of philosophy. Into what soil are the roots of metaphysics plunged?[28] This question implies that Descartes has not thought his simile quite through, and hence has left the roots of philosophy ungrounded. Within the setting of his own theory of wisdom, however, the situation has a different look.

28.   Martin Heidegger, *What Is Metaphysics?* Introduction: "The Way Back into the Ground of Metaphysics," trans. in W. Kaufmann, *Existentialism from Dostoevsky to Sartre* (New York: Meridian Books, 1956), p. 207.

Philosophical wisdom depends upon the act of intellectual recognition of certain truths as being the principles for an entire philosophy. This recognition is guided by the norm of looking for evidence which is indubitable, intuitively apprehended, and deductively fruitful of consequences. As Descartes views it, the norm specifies both the philosophical rooting and the soil into which the roots are sunk for nourishment. The basic propositions *about* the existing, thinking self rest upon a methodically tested sight *of* the self in its existential act. Moreover, the being of the self is dynamically conceived as bearing an intrinsic inclination toward the fullness of wisdom or *bona mens.* Philosophy is therefore rooted in a soil already richly endowed with the seeds of wisdom, so that there is a purposive continuity between the soil, the metaphysical roots, and the ultimate fruits of the one tree of wisdom. The real quarrel between Descartes and Heidegger concerns whether or not to include the human self and God among the strict principles of metaphysics.

Moral wisdom. Both in his definition of wisdom and in the image of the tree of philosophy, Descartes gives special mention to moral philosophy and the moral life as comprising the supreme moment of natural human wisdom. Medicine and mechanics are restricted wisdoms concerned with human health and control over nature, but moral philosophy shares in the unqualified meaning of wisdom because it aids man himself toward his proper good and happiness. There is a strictly mutual relationship between the speculative and the practical phases of philosophy. The speculative inquiries are intended ultimately to issue in some morally relevant truths, whereas moral philosophy draws its strength and direction from the foundation laid down in metaphysics and philosophy of nature. Only out of this close relationship can there develop a moral wisdom which rises above the specialized skills in order to direct man toward his sovereign natural good.

In developing the figure of the tree of philosophy, Descartes is careful to say that human wisdom reaches its climax not just in moral maxims but in moral science considered in its most perfect condition. Behind this qualification lies his distinction between the provisional rules of morality and the definitive moral philosophy, a distinction which is drawn and explained primarily in function of the theory of wisdom. What makes a natural moral teaching provisional or definitive is its relationship with the body of philosophical wisdom. If the teaching is formulated apart from the principles constituting Cartesian philosophical wisdom, then it must remain fundamentally provisional. Only a moral doctrine which is the outgrowth of such principles can be incorporated within the body of wisdom and thus serve as a definitive moral philosophy. This distinction is not intended to affect any moral teaching based upon revelation, but it does provide Descartes with a touchstone for determining the provisional or definitive character of our natural moral reasoning and moral maxims.

Where his general theory of wisdom is

most helpful is in showing the legitimacy
of provisional rules of morality and the
nature of the transition from a provisional
to a definitive moral outlook. Here, Descartes uses the same continuity-discontinuity principle already found so effective in
treating the degrees of wisdom. It enables
him to avoid the two extremes of a purely
conventional morality and outright Skepticism in the moral order. The Cartesian
middle way in moral philosophy is to ad-
vise us to regulate the rational character
of our adherence to moral rules strictly in
proportion to the particular stage at which
we find ourselves along the long route to
wisdom. If our minds are being guided
only by the lesser degrees of wisdom, then
our power and obligation are proportioned
to the provisional method of accepting the
common moral precepts and customs, without subjecting them to radical doubt.

> While we only possess the knowl-
> edges which are acquired by the first
> four degrees of wisdom, we should
> not doubt those things that appear to
> be true in what concerns the conduct

> of life, while yet we should not hold them to be so certain that we may not change our minds regarding them when obliged to do so by the evidence of some reason.[29]

As long as our basis in knowledge for ascertaining the moral good is still prephilosophical, the provisional standpoint is the morally appropriate and binding one.

This provisional approach is not purely conventional and pragmatic, however, since there are some active tendencies in the lower stages of wisdom which prompt us toward the genuine supreme natural good of man and hence toward the kind of knowledge upon which we can build our reasoned assent thereto. As long as we continue the search for philosophical wisdom and thus recognize the need for placing our moral assents eventually upon a philosophically evidenced footing, we are justified in taking the provisional standpoint. Every step in the reconstruction of a speculative knowledge through the method of

29. *Principles of Philosophy,* Preface (Haldane-Ross, I, 207, modified).

doubt will then be internally ordained toward an eventual transformation of our moral assent from the provisional to the definitive condition. Thus the transition from the one moral situation to the other is viewed by Descartes as a particular instance governed, and yet also guaranteed, by the more comprehensive transition from the preliminary wisdoms to the definitive human wisdom of philosophy.

Descartes chooses his words very carefully in describing moral wisdom. He speaks about it as "the most exalted knowledge of which the human mind is capable. . . . that highest point of wisdom in which the sovereign good of the life of man consists. . . . and this sovereign good, considered by the natural reason without the light of faith."[30] Cartesian moral wisdom is

30. *Ibid.* (Haldane-Ross, I, 205, 208, 209). The intimate link between Cartesian moral philosophy and the theory of wisdom is observed by P. Mesnard, *Essai sur la morale de Descartes* (Paris: Boivin, 1936), p. 222, and G. Rodis-Lewis, *La Morale de Descartes* (Paris: Presses Universitaires, 1957), pp. 121-24. Both authors also stress the limits placed by Descartes upon human wis-

an intellectual and a moral virtue. It gives a knowledge about man in relation to God and the natural course of events which the understanding can perceive and the will can assent to firmly in its truth. Drawing out the humanly important implications of the principles established in metaphysics and philosophy of nature, the wise man is enabled to take a steady, reflective view of his own composite nature, his involvement in the contingencies and necessities of the material world, and the providential ordering of himself and all temporal happenings by the wise and good God. This relational appreciation of the complex human situation in the light of divine providence constitutes *bona mens* or the proper perfection of the human mind in this world. It is a perfecting both of moral science in its definitive philosophical form and of the individual moral agent in his search for temporal felicity.

dom and its distinction from man's ultimate beatitude. The topic of intellectual limits is explored in chapter three of J. Laporte's *Le Rationalisme de Descartes* (2d ed.; Paris: Presses Universitaires, 1950).

In Descartes' estimation, his conception of moral wisdom surpasses the current teachings of the Stoics and Skeptics on wisdom. For one thing, he furnishes a basis in morally relevant metaphysical truths which these other thinkers lacked, either because they confused a physical with a metaphysical approach to God and the soul or because they were infected with Skepticism about all speculative truths. Moreover, the Cartesian view of moral wisdom is designed to bring a man joy as well as virtue, felicity as well as fortitude. A sapiential understanding of man, nature, and providence assures us of the superiority of the human mind to the entire material world, enables us to treat all temporal happenings as being ultimately subject to the moral will of God, and encourages us to love God in a relation of friendship. Our temporal felicity consists in controlling our passions and shaping our actions in accord with this complex relationship of which moral wisdom makes us aware.

Finally, Cartesian moral wisdom is presented as a natural and humanistic strengthening of the mind which does not lead to naturalism. There are definite limits to the knowledge and felicity which it brings to a man. It is here that Descartes reminds us forcefully that he has been developing the theme of the degrees of *human wisdom,* or the kind of comprehensive knowledge which comes naturally within our scope as men. He never revokes his basic axiom that universal human wisdom remains one and the same, and hence he never identifies human wisdom simply with wisdom as such. Precisely because human wisdom remains fundamentally the same in its certitude, continuity, and inherent limits, it cannot be confused either with God's own wisdom or with a religious wisdom based upon a revelation freely given to men by God. There are truths involving the divine infinity and freedom which transcend the limits of our natural intelligence, and yet which God may reveal to us as a distinct and superior wisdom. Hence the Cartesian theory of the degrees of human wisdom and its proportionate temporal felicity is not intended to engulf the religious wisdom and the beatitude which depend upon God's initiative in revelation.

Religious wisdom. There is not an internally generated continuity between religious wisdom and natural human wisdom, comprising philosophical wisdom and the four lower degrees. These latter degrees are eventually incorporated as subordinate aspects within philosophical wisdom, through the operation of a homogeneous method of reflection and a continuous path of intuitions and deductions. But religious wisdom does not share the same destiny with the lesser degrees of human wisdom. Descartes remarks that it comes to us with one stroke from the revealing God, insofar as we respond with the act of faith to His message. Religious wisdom is not therefore a systematic prolongation of our natural dynamism toward wisdom, but comes to us as a free gift from God. It never becomes a subordinate meaning within human wisdom, but remains an independent source of sapiential truth.

In treating of religious wisdom, then, Descartes exchanges his continuity-discontinuity principle for one of discontinuity, at least as far as concerns the foundation of the actual knowledge constituting this wisdom. This enables him to elaborate the topic of wisdom without leading to its complete naturalization, which was the aim of the freethinking Skeptics. When it is a question of founding evidence, he seeks to maintain the double autonomy of religious wisdom on a revelational basis and of human wisdom on a philosophically controlled basis. Descartes does not want theological considerations to intervene in constructing the house of human wisdom, and neither does he want the method and order of human wisdom to impose themselves upon the nature of religious wisdom and thus destroy its supernatural character.

When there is question of these two wisdoms in their ultimate forms, they must be developed by following two distinct and strictly irreducible pathways. Natural reason operates without the light of faith to yield human philosophical wisdom, and

the act of faith itself raises us to the certitudinal knowledge of religious wisdom
without the aid of philosophy. Once this
fundamental distinction is admitted on
the side of the founding acts for each wisdom, Descartes will then allow relation-
ships to grow up between the ultimate
knowledges in philosophy and religion.
He regards his own philosophical wisdom
as furnishing the best natural defense and
clarification of revealed truths. He is also
confident that immortality and other humanly important issues which philosophy
cannot demonstrate nevertheless are re-
solved with certainty in the teaching of
religious wisdom.[31]

There are two respects in which Descartes is not sufficiently critical of the wisdom doctrines prevalent at his time. The
first point concerns his manner of distinguishing between philosophical and religious wisdoms by stating that the light

31. The way in which Descartes treats of immor-
     tality within a sapiential context is described by
     J. Russier, *Sagesse cartésienne et religion* (Paris:
     Presses Universitaires, 1958).

of faith is not present in the former instance and is present in the latter. He has no way of achieving control over this criterion of the absence or presence of the light of faith, if it refers to a condition on the side of the individual inquiring mind. There is nothing in his philosophical method which enables him to determine a question of this sort. For that method concerns the test for clear and distinct evidence, but not the actual differentiation among the kinds of intellectual light which may be present in the investigator.

Stemming out of this shortcoming is a second one. Like many Christian Stoics and Skeptics, Descartes locates religious wisdom in faith and the gift of the Holy Spirit in such a way as to exclude a distinct theological type of wisdom. In defending the revealed basis and infallible certitude of religious faith and its gift of wisdom, he fails to recognize theological wisdom as a distinctive science and wisdom. Philosophy can aid the separately grounded religious wisdom and in this way perform some theological functions, but there is no room for a distinctively organized wisdom of theology. Since he always defines scientific knowledge as a study of first principles, Descartes fears that the admission of theological science as a type of wisdom would endanger his philosophical wisdom. Because he conceives of the relationship between philosophy and theology as that between rivals for the primacy of defining first principles, he has no resources for viewing their relation as a positive cooperation between distinctly founded and structured wisdoms.

What cannot be denied, however, is that Descartes was deeply challenged by the problem of wisdom in all its aspects. His response was not the perfunctory one of eulogy for a commonplace ideal, but the critical one of overhauling most of the elements in that ideal and putting them to the test. Those elements which survived critical inspection were then refashioned in ways dictated by his own conception of the method and order of philosophical reasoning. The result was a well articulated doctrine on wisdom which displayed

its systematic connections with the rest of
the Cartesian philosophy and attempted
to meet the desire of men to share in wisdom, even under conditions of skeptical
questioning and social upheaval.

3. PHILOSOPHICAL WISDOM TODAY

Anyone who attempts to engage today
in the search for wisdom soon discovers
that the situation is not entirely different
from that which confronted men at the
beginning of the modern age. There is still
a deep spontaneous desire among men of
all conditions for sharing in the insight and
stability which wisdom brings along with
it. And there is still a sharp division of
opinion among reflective minds about
whether human wisdom is ever attainable,
especially in its philosophical form. The
best procedure for those seeking a philosophical estimation of the prospects for
wisdom in our age is to move the analysis
quickly from the plane of vague general
commendations and predictions to that of
particular considerations. There are several definite steps which can be taken to-

ward understanding the factors in the problem itself and removing some of the difficulties presently blocking the realization of the ideal of wisdom among men.

1) One purpose of our historical discussion is to indicate the need for more intensive historical studies of the whole development of the question of wisdom. Descartes is only one example of a major thinker who devoted considerable attention to it and tried to give it an answer meeting his own requirements for philosophical rigor. The vein of philosophical thought on wisdom has to be mined patiently and skillfully, since it does not lie upon the surface. What the great philosophers have said about wisdom may seem at first glance to be banal and easily removed from the main line of their thought. But the closer we read the sources, the better we can see that this first impression is misleading and is probably due to the trivialized form in which we hold our own views on wisdom. When we make the actual effort to analyze the theory of wisdom in a major philosopher of the stature of

Aristotle or Aquinas or Kant, we find that it cannot be detached from the main doctrines and cannot be interpreted properly without constant reference to them. It is not reasonable to expect, then, that there will be vital consideration of the problem of wisdom today until we cease to be historically estranged from the rich contributions made to it by great philosophers in every age.

On the particular point of the modernity of the theme of wisdom, however, the objection may well be advanced that Descartes' preoccupation with it is one more indication of the medieval rather than the modern cast of his mind. The implied premise behind this argument is that familiarity with the state of a question among the medievals and the Renaissance writers is incompatible with giving the issue a modern treatment. But ignorance of the drift of previous discussions of a topic should not be taken as a defining note of the modern approach in philosophy. What counts is the manner of relating one's mind to the philosophical tradition. Descartes

was familiar with many aspects of the tradition on wisdom, but he was also fundamentally dissatisfied with the previous accounts and regarded a new foundation for
the theory of wisdom as one of his indispensable goals in philosophy. Thereby, he
did his share toward assuring that modern
philosophers would continue to treat the
ideal of wisdom as a challenge, calling for
their best professional effort in response.

To show that they have actually so re-
sponded would amount to developing the
history of the idea of wisdom in post-Car-
tesian philosophy. For instance, one way
of asking new questions about Spinoza and
Locke and thus of gaining a fresh vision of
their significance would be to examine
their positions on the attainability of human wisdom. Spinoza would then emerge
as a sapiential thinker who wanted an even
closer relationship than did Descartes between metaphysical and ethical wisdom,
and whose tightly sealed naturalism displayed itself quite consistently in his re-
fusal to accept the Cartesian thesis about
a nonphilosophical religious wisdom. And

Locke's remarks on the contentment of the human mind to remain within the limits of a very few certitudes and a vast ocean of probable practical beliefs would be seen as a counterimage of wisdom, one of the most powerful modern conceptions of the knowledge proper to the humanly wise man. The tensions behind Locke and the rationalists could then be used as helpful background for understanding the clash between Kant and Hegel over the meaning and realizability of the ideal of human wisdom. Crowding closer to our own time would be the joyful wisdom of Nietzsche, the evolutionists' wisdom of the life process, and the social wisdom sought after in democratic decision making.

2) The historical persistence and prominence of the wisdom theme in modern philosophy provide no guarantee of its having a similar role in contemporary thought. No great human ideal is exempt from the danger of being effectively repudiated under criticism or simply of eroding away in the press of new methods and goals for research. Wisdom is just as vul-

nerable as any other major aim of human
effort, and in point of fact it does stand
under trial today, at least as far as the professional philosophers are concerned.
There is, indeed, a widely supported informal conviction in our society that long
human experience and eminence of
achievement in particular fields bring
along with them a practical wisdom which
it is valuable for us to consult.[32] Yet there
is little agreement among philosophers
that their discipline can yield a rigorously
tested speculative and practical wisdom.
The paradoxical situation is that those
thinkers who seem most committed to
wisdom by the nature of their intellectual
work are nevertheless the least sure of
whether men can attain it or even should
desire to attain it.

32. For instance, see the magazine *Wisdom*, bearing as its subtitle: "the magazine of knowledge
for all America," and featuring excerpts from the
writings of Shaw and Maugham, Einstein and
Schweitzer, Lincoln and Churchill. Also, John
Nef, *Civilization, Industrial Society, and Love*
(Santa Barbara: Center for the Study of Democratic Institutions, 1961), pp. 11-12, and other

The roots of this basic hesitancy among philosophers about the traditional view of their vocation are complex and difficult to trace out. One consideration is shared by almost everyone working in the field, namely, that wisdom cannot be made an exception to the program of inquiry. The validity and feasibility of the ideal of wisdom must be put to the test, although not necessarily in a skeptical spirit which would preclude any eventual reaffirmation of its soundness. I regard acceptance of this condition as basic for any philosophical treatment of wisdom, since there are no privileged regions in philosophy. It is legitimate to demand that a contemporary way be found for showing that wisdom has a definite meaning, that it can come within reach of our methods of investigation, and that it is worth striving after.

Sometimes, it is felt antecedently, however, that the philosopher has no business even discussing the problem of wisdom.

publications of this Center stressing the political importance of knowledge in the form of moral and religious wisdom.

The word "wisdom" jars on many philo-sophically sensitive ears today, because of a connotation suggesting that the posses-sor of wisdom has special access to an eso-teric source of insight enabling him to re-solve easily all our speculative and prac-tical matters of dispute. The pretentious nature of this claim then leads many minds to repudiate the wisdom theme itself and confine philosophy resolutely to piecework production, where there can be no ques-tion of a grandiose knowledge of all things in their highest causes.

Doubtless, a sharp restriction of the range of one's philosophical analysis is the most effective way to preserve intellectual modesty and deflate the swollen concep-tion sometimes entertained of wisdom. In doing so, however, it is important to avoid two extremes which can easily attend upon the process of analytic deflation. One such extreme is to infer from the success of making restricted investigations that the philosopher should refrain in principle from raising such a broad question as that of wisdom. This is an inverse type of ex-

aggeration about the scope of philosophizing, and it prejudges the issue instead of
finding out whether or not there are ways
of controlling the discussion of wisdom.

A second uncritical inference would
be to suppose, without some direct examination of the question, that every notion of wisdom conforms to the connotation under attack. The unspoken premise
here is that, in method and content, the
theory of wisdom stands opposed to our
ordinary use of intelligence, our body of
well ascertained knowledge, and our
strong awareness of limitations in human
studies. This premise cannot stand up
under a historically well informed scrutiny.
There are some widely divergent conceptions of wisdom in Western thought, but
most of those which are developed philosophically agree at least in denying the
supposed opposition. Our example of Descartes shows that a sustained effort is made
to determine the meaning of wisdom in
accord with the common method of inquiry, to present it as the unifying peak of
human knowledges, and to take specific

account of the limitations of the human mind in attaining to it. Whatever we may think about the soundness of the particular attempts to show the solidarity between science and wisdom, the pattern of the investigation is firmly enough established to rule out the assumption that the pursuit of wisdom always entails a groundless claim to esoteric understanding beyond the real scope of man's mind.

3) In order to make the question of wisdom pertinent to our other contemporary concerns in philosophy, it is helpful to make use of the two current methods of analysis of ordinary language and phenomenological description in the broad sense. These procedures are particularly apt for enlivening two aspects of the theory of wisdom which have become deadened through sheer repetition of the classical teaching. The two aspects in question are the discussion of the traits of the wise man and the distinction made between restricted and unqualified forms of wisdom. Usually, these portions of the theory of wisdom are hurried over as being of very

minor importance and interest to philosophers. Yet they do touch upon some deep
concerns today, and they do lend themselves to treatment by philosophical methods now widely in use. The opportunity
should not be lost of posing the question
about wisdom in an area and a manner
that are quite meaningful to contemporary
minds.

Certainly, Aristotle's analysis of the
characteristic traits of the wise man is noteworthy for its relevance to his own situation.[33] Taking full advantage of Plato's
hard-won distinction between the sophist
and the lover of wisdom, Aristotle thinks
it important to make a concrete sketch of

33. "Metaphysics," I, 2, 982a4-20, in *The Basic
    Works of Aristotle*, ed. R. McKeon (New York:
    Random House, 1941), p. 691. St. Thomas con-
    denses the portrait of the wise men into this
    sentence: "The wise man is described as one
    who knows all, even difficult matters, with certi-
    tude and through their cause; who seeks this
    knowledge for its own sake; and who directs
    others and induces them to act." *Commentary on
    the Metaphysics of Aristotle*, book I, lesson 2,
    number 43, trans. J. P. Rowan (2 vols.; Chicago:
    Henry Regnery, 1961), I, 19.

the latter. He listens attentively to ordinary talk in the Athenian community in order to determine what people commonly attribute to men whom they regard as wise. He is as careful here to be responsive to common discourse as he is when developing the theory of the categories and that of the moral virtues. As the description of the wise man is gradually filled in, two definite purposes are achieved. Through this inductive approach, we are reminded that wisdom dwells among us in concrete human form and hence that any theory about it must respect the ways and limits of the human mind. At the same time, Aristotle is using the empirical materials as a philosopher and not simply as a reporter. He orders this study of common usage so that it will prepare people to accept his own theory about the metaphysical sort of wisdom. Thus the wise man's habit of seeking the broad principles which order our other knowledges is interpreted as referring primarily to a search for causal explanatory principles. Similarly, in St. Thomas' commentary on this passage there is a philosophical ordering of the analysis of the wise man, in order to lead us gradually toward acceptance of speculative and practical judging in reference to God as being the characteristic operation of the mind strengthened by wisdom.

In the Northern Renaissance, Justus Lipsius saw the philosophical advantages of developing the theme of the wise man. It furnished him with a way of showing the basic agreement between the common opinion on wisdom and the Stoic ethical doctrine. Lipsius also argued that, if we perceive the soundness of this portrait of the wise man (as formally stated in Stoic terms and as amended in the light of Christian belief), then we should also be prepared to recognize that the rigorous justification of wisdom rests upon the Stoic logic, physics, and ethics. Thus Lipsius sought to strengthen the case for his own philosophy by the indirect means of showing its contribution toward validating and realizing the ideal of the wise man. Again, within Spinoza's system, this topic was assigned the crucial function of further orienting and encouraging the individual mind which is beginning to devote itself to the search after God. By keeping before it some definite pattern of wise living, such a mind can persevere in its struggle with the passions and thus increase its virtue or intrinsic power of acting.

There are always fresh virtualities to discover in making an analysis of the common view of the ideal of wisdom. And especially at a time when there is considerable questioning among philosophers themselves about the value and practicability of this ideal, it is also advisable to pay closer attention to the distinction between the qualified and plenary meanings for wisdom. The purpose of this distinction is not merely the negative one of denying that metaphysical and moral wisdoms are the same as the restricted kinds of wisdom. There is also the positive aim of discovering the core of common meaning for wisdom which is present in the restricted forms, as well as that of determining how to integrate the several wisdoms of man. This latter problem does not concern sole-

ly the general wisdoms but also their relationship with the qualified wisdoms,
which should not be neglected and left in
meaningless isolation. When the problem
of human wisdom is stated in its full human complexity, we realize the need for
beginning our inductive analysis with the
restricted types of wisdom and for including them in the effort at unifying the several wisdoms of man.

The value of making a comparative
study of both levels of wisdom is one historical lesson which can be drawn from
the Cartesian theory of the degrees of wisdom. The example of Descartes is sufficient warning that a philosophically developed doctrine on wisdom cannot afford
to pass hurriedly over the particularized
modes of wisdom. It is necessary to ex-
plore what qualities of mind are required
in order to have a man regarded as a wise
statesman or physician or judge. To determine at least some of the qualities of
the wise man in these restricted areas helps
to bring out the experiential basis for our
common conviction about the capacity and

desire of men to become wise. Such analyses give us a measure of encouragement that wisdom is not entirely beyond our reach and that we have some guidance for developing its more inclusive forms. And today, the philosopher can use the resources of psychological and sociological studies concerned with the professions and their social significance. With their aid, he can give a more pertinent account of the factor of difficulty involved in the attainment of outstanding knowledge in any field, the precise meaning of seasoned judgment as a trait which makes a man not merely a specialist but an experienced and balanced specialist, and the way in which a man of seasoned judgment in one area tends to have some authority even in matters of general human concern. By making the basis of discussion of wisdom as wide and scientifically informed as possible, its lure can be felt more deeply and established more satisfactorily.

The danger with this course is that we may become so enamored with the restricted modes of wisdom that we will mistake them for wisdom in its fullness and thus abandon the search for metaphysical, moral, and religious forms of wisdom. Gabriel Marcel has this possible outcome in mind when he warns against the dissolution and decline of wisdom in our civilization.[34] There are strong pressures encouraging men to concentrate all their energy and valuation upon the specialized areas of knowledge and skill. Then the plenary ideal of viewing all our actions, values, and ways of knowing in the light of their common reference to God tends to grow dim and disappear for lack of actual cultivation. Natural philosophical wisdom and religious wisdom are threatened by the specializing demands made upon our intelligence and by the manipulative attitude taken toward all values in nature and society. It is difficult to be wise in the unrestricted sense in a world where only the limited and instrumental significance of men and things is permitted to attract our minds.

34.   Gabriel Marcel, *The Decline of Wisdom* (New York: Philosophical Library, 1955), pp. 37ff.

Yet it seems to me that this danger only reinforces the need of examining more in depth the relationship between the restricted and the general meanings for wisdom. For this is one way of finding out how to unify the humanistic and scientific knowledges, as well as the technological and personal aspects of practical existence. The problem of such integration is basically a problem in the relationship among the several forms of wisdom. To see the issue in this perspective is to discern some bonds of analogy among the kinds of wisdom, and thus also to prepare the personal ground for drawing them together.

4) One firm conclusion emerging from our historical study is that the theory of wisdom is controlled by the rest of one's philosophy, especially by one's position on metaphysics. If the Cartesian theory of wisdom differs from the Stoic, Skeptic, and Spinozistic versions, that is because Descartes shapes his doctrine on wisdom in function of his own views on method and metaphysical knowledge. This relationship suggests that a certain order must be re-

spected in presenting the conception of wisdom. It does not prove effective in philosophy to begin with a full-scale formal *doctrine* on wisdom, since such a doctrine depends for its understanding and acceptance upon other issues which have not yet been treated. Where we can very well make our start, however, is with a *love* of wisdom, with a concrete conception of wisdom as a human ideal which is supremely worthy of our pursuit. What is important at the outset of philosophical inquiry is not a set definition of wisdom but an image of the wise man and a love of sharing in his perfection of mind. Once we do set our feet upon the pathway toward wisdom, then we can see the connection between this quest and the particular philosophical inquiries concerning the nature and limits of human knowledge, the composite being of man and its causal source, and the order among the goods sought by men. Out of a careful examination of these questions, we can then prepare the foundation for a verified doctrine on wisdom.

Especially in trying to develop a con-

temporary philosophical theory of wisdom
that uses the resources of St. Thomas, it
is necessary to examine the relationship between the initial love of wisdom and that
love of wisdom which springs from a sub-
stantiated doctrine thereon.[35] The transition from the one to the other sort of hold
upon wisdom is effected by what may be
called *the method of metaphysical ingression,* or a progressive penetration into the
metaphysical bases for the ideal of wisdom.

It begins with a critique of the isolated
way of presenting the theory of wisdom.
We are often confronted at once with the
culminating definition of metaphysical
wisdom as a speculative intellectual virtue
inclining the mind to judge and order all
things with certainty in respect to their
supreme causes and principles, especially

35. The connection established by Aquinas between wisdom, love, and beatitude is explained
in E. Gilson, *Wisdom and Love in St. Thomas
Aquinas* ("The Aquinas Lectures" [Milwaukee:
Marquette University Press, 1951]). For the
main points in the Thomistic theory of wisdom,
cf. C. A. Lofy, S.J., *The Virtue of Wisdom in
Selected Texts of Saint Thomas* (unpublished
Master's thesis, Saint Louis University, 1956).

God. When proposed in this abrupt and isolated way, this conception of wisdom is likely to strike the unprepared mind as being no more than a remote and unsupported wish for gaining a higher sort of knowledge. Such a mind is not dissatisfied with any particular element in the definition, but rather with the entire situation of being confronted at the outset with a view of wisdom which calls for one's immediate acceptance or rejection as to its truth. The point of the criticism is that a person cannot fairly be expected to judge at once concerning the truth of a terminal definition of wisdom. Metaphysical wisdom does not come to the searcher in a flash and apart entirely from a carefully elaborated context of inferences, and neither should it be proposed to anyone else entirely apart from reference to its real context of evidence and inferences. It is doing a disservice to this intellectual virtue to make acceptance of its reality depend mainly upon an understanding of the terms used in its definition. Perhaps of all the virtues in the intellectual order, wisdom requires the most patient preparatory discussion and the most careful correlation with the actual state of judgment on the part of the inquiring mind.

It is better to regard the above account of wisdom as being at the outset, a description of a goal to be sought or a proposal about a kind of knowledge whose conditions must now be investigated and tested. We can then notice the common operational factor in the description of the wise man in some particular field and that of the man who is called wise in respect to philosophical generality. In both instances, emphasis is placed upon the confident ability to judge and order matters falling within the wise man's competence. In the case of a proposed metaphysical wisdom, this means an ability to judge and order all the kinds of beings and knowledges which are available to man. To back up such a large claim, some grounds must be produced for being able to engage in this judicative and ordinative work. A philosopher can do so with confidence and authority only on condition of his possessing a certitude of knowledge about things in their causes and being-aspect, and about knowledge in its own nature and principles.

Thus the method of metaphysical ingression forces us to shift attention from the operational consequences to the source of their activity, from the sapiential work of judging and ordering back to the certitudinal knowledge underlying this work. In order to establish a philosophical theory of metaphysical wisdom, explicit reference must be made to the grounds in knowledge for the certitude characterizing the mind of the man of such wisdom. This part of the analysis is made in two stages, the first of which concerns our philosophical knowledge about God and the other our knowledge of first principles of being and knowing.

Knowledge in the wisdom mode has a universal import, not because the wise man's mind is encyclopedic in range, but because it considers the various ways of being and knowing in terms of their common reference to God as the first causal

existent. Metaphysical wisdom (as distinct
from theological) enables us to judge and
order on the basis of that sort of knowledge about God which we obtain by inference from experienced beings. Thus the
full weight of the problem of metaphysical
wisdom centers upon the causal inference
to God, since this inference specifies the
distinctive kind of certitude and causal explanation required for a metaphysical way
of judging and ordering things. It is helpful to describe the meaning whereby we
may intend the reality of God, but eventually the method of metaphysical ingression
leads beyond descriptive analysis to the
question of the actual demonstration of
the truth of the proposition about the existing, causing God. This method entails a
more radical questioning about the
grounds of certitude for our propositions
on God than can be satisfied by phenomenological description or analytical elucidation taken alone.[36]

36. Cf. Joseph Owens, C.Ss.R., "St. Thomas and
Elucidation," *The New Scholasticism*, XXXV
(1961), 421-44, and James Collins, "The Re-

The ingressive method also requires us
to become explicit about the other distinctive trait of metaphysical wisdom: its task
of analyzing and defending the principles
of human knowledge and inference, including the inference concerning God. The
man whose wisdom is in the metaphysical
mode has the unique office of probing into
the meaning, the experiential evidence,
and the ways of defense for the unrestricted principles of human knowledge
and real being. In this function, metaphysical wisdom is distinguished from all
other forms of wisdom and also from the

ligious Theme in Existentialism," in *Philosophy
and the Modern Mind,* ed. F. X. Canfield (De-
troit: Sacred Heart Seminary, 1961), pp. 20-48.
Edmund Husserl distinguished sharply between
phenomenology as a rigorously scientific philosophy and the various wisdom philosophies, which
he regarded as historical unifications of a particular outlook rather than as well-founded knowledge. Wisdom is a valid way of unifying cultural
values only until the phenomenological ideal of
philosophy as a strict science is introduced. See
Edmund Husserl, "Philosophy as a Strict Science,"
Cross Currents, VI (1956), 336-44. Yet in his
final period Husserl sometimes referred broadly
to his philosophy as saving the values of wisdom.

other speculative intellectual virtues of understanding and science. Whether metaphysical wisdom is regarded by itself or in the context of its use by theological and moral wisdoms, it has the distinctive responsibility of inspecting, verifying, and guarding the true propositions concerning the principle of contradiction, the meaning and act of existence, and the bearing of sense perception upon our experience of existent beings. The meaning and evidence for these common principles of all human knowledge are reflectively ascertained, and their bearing upon the causal inference to God determined, by the human mind insofar as it is responsive to the habit of metaphysical wisdom.

By means of this metaphysical ingression, then, we are gradually led to recognize the twofold foundation for the judging and ordering acts of metaphysical wisdom. These functions can be performed in a metaphysically legitimate way, provided that the judging and ordering intellect has the certitude of knowledge drawn from its causal inference to God and its reflective inspection of the import and direct evidence for the first principles or resolutive basis of human knowledge. Once this condition is stated, the theory of wisdom can include a reference to God and a certain kind of universal consideration of other things, without failing to respect the limitations of human inquiry and its distinctive genesis. Thus qualified, the theistic conception of metaphysical wisdom has nothing esoteric and inflated about it. The difficulties which it raises remain squarely within the range of settlement through human discussion.

5) The modern history of the topic of wisdom is sufficiently instructive to induce contemporary Thomists to develop an explicit doctrine on moral wisdom. The materials for such a doctrine are present in St. Thomas himself, and the incentive for undertaking the necessary philosophical rethinking of the issues is provided by the actual course of modern analyses of wisdom.[37] From the early Renaissance onward,

37. The Thomistic texts are discussed by V. J. Bourke, "The Role of a Proposed Practical In-

there has been no hesitation among philosophers about dealing with the question of a moral sort of human wisdom. Moreover, they have deliberately faced the question of whether man's quest of the good can be regulated entirely by a natural virtue of moral wisdom. The issue is now formally a portion of the philosophical tradition on wisdom, and this historical step cannot be revoked. It is only after working out in detail the nature and scope of a natural moral wisdom that the distinction can be drawn significantly in philosophy between the integrity of this habit and its limitations for ordering our search after happiness. The limitations inherent in a philosophically established moral wisdom were acknowledged by such theistic philosophers as Descartes and Locke, and were attacked by Spinoza and subsequent naturalists. Present-day philosophical contributions to this controverted matter can best

tellectual Virtue of Wisdom," *Proceedings of the American Catholic Philosophical Association*, XXVI (1952), 160-67, with comments by L. H. Kendzierski (168-79).

be made by developing a philosophical theory of moral wisdom which is well informed about the arguments advanced since Siger of Brabant's time.

A cognate issue which has been considerably sharpened by modern reflections on wisdom is the distinction between moral wisdom considered as the climax of moral science and as a perfection of the individual moral agent. One of Descartes' chief preoccupations throughout his treatment of wisdom is to achieve the passage from provisional morality to moral wisdom, both in the sense of securing a demonstrative basis for moral doctrine and in that of strengthening the moral agent. The Cartesian tree of wisdom flowers into a moral wisdom on the part of the prudent man, because he can now draw upon a moral philosophy which itself rests upon well established principles. This double insistence is also found in Spinoza and Leibniz, Kant and Bergson, each developing it in a characteristic way.

The distinction is operative not only historically but also in any assessment of the present prospects for wisdom. The common expectancy of finding some sort of moral wisdom among experienced men usually refers more pertinently to the personal wisdom of the sage man than to the wisdom of a moral science. Whatever the clashes among systems of ethics, there is still a strong hope that practical experience and responsible use of power will bring along with them a growth in moral wisdom on the individual's part. An adequate theory about wisdom will have to take account of this distinction and the somewhat despairing interpretation made of it in the face of the conflict among ethical theories.

In attempting to realize moral wisdom in its full actuality as regulating doctrine, method, and individual judgment, philosophers must face the further question of whether this integral conception is possible without some metaphysical groundwork. Except for those who may still regard the positivist criticism of metaphysics as definitive, this is a genuine problem. Even Kant found it necessary to determine some metaphysical principles for ethics, within the context of his own meaning for such principles, as well as to reaffirm the ideal of the morally wise man.

John Dewey wrestled with this issue throughout his Carus Lectures on *Experience and Nature*. He was ready enough to regard philosophy itself as a pursuit of wisdom, more especially of moral wisdom as a disciplined way of acting in our precarious universe. Indeed, he distinguished between true and false wisdom on the basis of whether or not a philosophy recognizes the need to put its knowledge of the natural world practically to work in enlightening and guiding our human action.

> A true wisdom, devoted to the latter task [of an opening and enlarging of the ways of nature in man], discovers in thoughtful observation and experiment the method of administering the unfinished processes of existence so that frail goods shall be substantiated, secure goods be extended, and the precarious promises of good that haunt experienced things be more liberally fulfilled.[38]

38.   John Dewey, *Experience and Nature* (reprint

By thus defining genuine wisdom so closely in terms of his own philosophical method, Dewey took his place among the wisdom thinkers and offered a predominantly
moral interpretation. He conceded a wisdom aspect to his metaphysical analysis
of the generic traits of existence only by
virtue of its ultimate reference to the concrete human situation, where values are
criticized and developed. In Dewey's explanation, philosophy is primarily a moral
wisdom, and metaphysical analysis shares
in wisdom only insofar as it contributes
toward the practical understanding, control, and enjoyment of human goods.

Thus from the time of Descartes and
Spinoza to that of Dewey and Whitehead,
modern philosophers have associated the

ed.; New York: Dover Press, 1958), pp. 76-77.
Kant has a rewarding discussion of wisdom and
the character of the wise man, in *Critique of
Practical Reason*, trans. L. W. Beck (New York:
Liberal Arts Press, 1956), p. 11, n. 9, and pp.
127-32. There is a contemporary idealistic analy-
sis of wisdom in terms of the rational temper, in
Brand Blanshard's *Reason and Goodness* (New
York: Macmillan, 1961), pp. 427 ff.

problem of moral wisdom with that of metaphysics. The relationship has been variously conceived as a Cartesian continuity of inference, a Spinozistic identification of metaphysics and moral wisdom, a Kantian supplanting of the former by the latter, and a Deweyan instrumental reference of the former to the latter. In any case, one requirement for participating in this discussion is to elaborate a philosophical theory of moral wisdom, so that questions of comparison and limitation can be treated in a definite manner. The welfare of metaphysical and religious wisdoms is just as much at stake here as is that of moral wisdom itself.

6) I would like to conclude with two recommendations suggested by the consistently prominent place assigned to the question of religious wisdom throughout the history of Western thought. First, the philosophical study of wisdom theories can be enriched by bringing to bear the resources of theology and comparative religion upon this question. Especially in utilizing the comparative approach, how-

ever, it is essential to heed the lesson of the history of wisdom and recognize the presence of a persistent wisdom tradition in the West as well as the East. There are no good historical grounds for accepting a sharp dichotomy between the scientific practical mind of Western man and the contemplative sapiential mind of Eastern man. The ideal of wisdom is a common human ideal which is supported by thinkers in all cultural climates and periods.[39] The Western stress upon rational explanation, scientific certainty, and practical control is not intended to be made at the expense of wisdom. For precisely one of the central themes developed by Western philosophers is the relation of culmination which wisdom bears toward rational explanation and scientific certainty, as well as the relation of ultimate guidance which it bears toward our technological and moral activities.

39.   This point is well made by M. C. D'Arcy, S.J., *The Meeting of Love and Knowledge* (New York: Harper, 1957), and by Jacques Maritain, *Science and Wisdom* (New York: Scribner, 1940), pp. 4-33.

An adequate account of human reflections on wisdom must be intercultural in nature, without proceeding on the crippling assumption that wisdom springs only from one cultural source. Even the notion that Western thought confines itself to the wisdom of nature, whereas the wisdoms of self and society must be sought after respectively in India and China, fails to work as a fruitful postulate. In every cultural situation, the theme of wisdom has been pursued through a complex reference to nature, self, and society. These are the great compass points, along with God, for charting the various meanings packed into the common human search after wisdom. There are degrees of emphasis and combination among these fundamental referents in the theory of wisdom, but in some way they are all implicated in the major conceptions formulated in East and West about the wise man.

Finally, the concern of the wisdom seekers is not only for synthesis and unification among the modes of wisdom, but also for appreciating their proper differences. The pluralism among the forms of wisdom is retained by all but the most resolute monists, and even the latter must accommodate the several forms in some dialectical way. A description of the common features of wisdom does not amount to a univocal definition, nor does an ordering among the kinds of wisdom mean that they are all reducible to one premier sort. The unity of wisdom remains thoroughly analogical, because the analogates or actual modes of wisdom to which it refers are themselves different sorts of habitual knowledge. Speculative wisdom does not cease to be itself, even when some practical use is made of its significance. And metaphysical wisdom retains its own nature as a distinctive kind of knowledge and certainty, even when it is being used in theological investigations. It is true that the wise man seeks to unify the human and divine wisdoms in his own life, but he does not do so by obliterating the actually different modes of knowing which remain even within his unity of purpose and love. This is a reminder, at the deepest point in our intellectual life, that we do not yet share in the visional union of all the wisdoms open to man. Remaining this side of a direct sharing in God's own integral wisdom, we must continue to be in pursuit of the unity of wisdom through its plural human modes. Hence, we must continue to regard it as an ideal not yet fully realized by us.

Wisdom presents itself to us not simply as a doctrine but as an ideal and a lure. In any responsible treatment, the attractiveness of wisdom must be fostered by keeping open its several forms and avenues of approach. For both theoretical and practical reasons, it is inadvisable to reduce everything immediately to the question of the ultimate unity of our wisdoms. This is premature from the philosophical side, since much work remains to be done both historically and analytically on the different kinds of knowledge which bring wisdom with them. And in the practical sphere, wisdom can exert its lure upon men only if they are taken in their actual condition and hence in their various ways of

conceiving it. They can learn to love and
seek it through reflection on ordinary experience and through formal study, by
way of metaphysical reflection and by way
of moral judgment, with the aid of theological science and with the aid of the gift
of the Holy Spirit present in men of faith.
Along each of these routes, men can gain
a genuine possession of wisdom. Hence all
the paths should be kept well swept and
inviting, even when we accept the long
range goal of working toward a critical
unification of the several wisdoms of man.
In this way, we can contribute our human
share toward the justifying of wisdom by
all her children.[40]

40.   The conception of wisdom in the Old Testa-
      ment is examined by R. E. Murphy, O.Carm.,
      Seven Books of Wisdom (Milwaukee: Bruce,
      1960). The Scriptural, as well as Greek sources
      of the ideal of wisdom are operative in the
      thought of the French philosopher, Félix Ravais-
      son. This is noticeable in the text edited by P.-M.
      Schuhl, "Une note inédite de Ravaisson sur la
      sagesse," *Revue Philosophique de France et de
      l'Étranger*, LXXXVI (1961), 89-90. For some re-

cent French discussion of wisdom in relation to
various sciences and acts of the mind, see *Les
sciences et la sagesse* (Paris: Presses Universitaires, 1950), including two essays on Carthesian
wisdom.

The Aquinas Lectures

Published by the Marquette University Press,
Milwaukee 3, Wisconsin

St. Thomas and the Life of Learning (1937) by
Fr. John F. McCormick, S.J., professor of
philosophy, Loyola University.

St. Thomas and the Gentiles (1938) by Morti-
mer J. Adler, Ph.D., director of the Institute
of Philosophical Research, San Francisco,
Calif.

St. Thomas and the Greeks (1939) by Anton C.
Pegis, Ph.D., professor of philosophy, Pontifical Institute of Mediaeval Studies, Toronto.

The Nature and Functions of Authority (1940)
by Yves Simon, Ph.D., professor of philosophy of social thought, University of Chicago.

St. Thomas and Analogy (1941) by Fr. Gerald
B. Phelan, Ph.D., professor of philosophy, St.
Michael's College, Toronto.

St. Thomas and the Problem of Evil (1942) by
Jacques Maritain, Ph.D., professor *emeritus*
of philosophy, Princeton University.

Humanism and Theology (1943) by Werner Jaeger, Ph.D., Litt.D., University professor, Harvard University.

The Nature and Origins of Scientism (1944) by John Wellmuth.

Cicero in the Courtroom of St. Thomas Aquinas (1945) by E. K. Rand, Ph.D., Litt.D., LL.D., Pope professor of Latin, *emeritus,* Harvard University.

St. Thomas and Epistemology (1946) by Fr. Louis-Marie Regis, O.P., Th.L., Ph.D., director of the Albert the Great Institute of Mediaeval Studies, University of Montreal.

St. Thomas and the Greek Moralists (1947, Spring) by Vernon J. Bourke, Ph.D., professor of philosophy, St. Louis University, St. Louis, Missouri.

History of Philosophy and Philosophical Education (1947, Fall) by Étienne Gilson of the *Académie française,* director of studies and professor of the history of Mediaeval philosophy, Pontifical Institute of Mediaeval Studies, Toronto.

The Natural Desire for God (1948) by Fr. William R. O'Connor, S.T.L., Ph.D., professor of dogmatic theology, St. Joseph's Seminary, Dunwoodie, N.Y.

St. Thomas and the World State (1949) by Robert M. Hutchins, Chancellor of the University of Chicago.

Method in Metaphysics (1950) by Fr. Robert J. Henle, S.J., dean of the graduate school, St. Louis University, St. Louis, Missouri.

Wisdom and Love in St. Thomas Aquinas (1951) by Étienne Gilson of the *Académie française*, director of studies and professor of the history of Mediaeval philosophy, Pontifical Institute of Mediaeval Studies, Toronto.

The Good in Existential Metaphysics (1952) by Elizabeth G. Salmon, associate professor of philosophy in the graduate school, Fordham University.

St. Thomas and the Object of Geometry (1953) by Vincent Edward Smith, Ph.D., professor of philosophy, University of Notre Dame.

Realism and Nominalism Revisited (1954) by Henry Veatch, Ph.D., professor of philosophy, Indiana University.

Imprudence in St. Thomas Aquinas (1955) by Charles J. O'Neil, Ph.D., professor of philosophy, Marquette University.

The Truth That Frees (1956) by Fr. Gerard Smith, S.J., Ph.D., professor and chairman of the department of philosophy, Marquette University.

St. Thomas and the Future of Metaphysics (1957) by Fr. Joseph Owens, C.Ss.R., associate professor of philosophy, Pontifical Institute of Mediaeval Studies, Toronto.

Thomas and the Physics of 1958: A Confrontation (1958) by Henry Margenau, Ph.D., Eugene Higgins professor of physics and natural philosophy, Yale University.

Metaphysics and Ideology (1959) by Wm. Oliver Martin, professor of philosophy, University of Rhode Island.

Language, Truth and Poetry (1960) by Victor M. Hamm, Ph.D., professor of English, Marquette University.

Metaphysics and Historicity (1961) by Emil L. Fackenheim, Ph.D., associate professor of philosophy, University of Toronto.

The Lure of Wisdom (1962) by James D. Collins, Ph.D., professor of philosophy, St. Louis University.

Uniform format, cover and binding.